Student Workbook for
EVOLUTION OF A GROUP

Gerald Corey
California State University, Fullerton

Marianne Schneider Corey
Consultant

Robert Haynes
Borderline Productions

Video directed by Thomas Walters
and produced by Robert Haynes

Brooks/Cole • Wadsworth
I(T)P® An International Thomson Publishing Company

Pacific Grove, CA • Albany, NY • Belmont, CA • Boston • Cincinnati • Johannesburg • London
Madrid • Melbourne • Mexico City • New York • Scottsdale, AZ • Singapore • Tokyo • Toronto

Executive Editor: Craig Barth
Counseling Editor: Eileen Murphy
Assistant Editor: Julie Martinez
Marketing Managers: Liz Poulsen and Jennie Burger
Project Editor: Howard Severson
Print Buyer: Stacey Weinberger
Copy Editing & Composition: Erick and Mary Ann Reinstedt
Cover and Box Design: Carole Lawson
Cover Photo: Dale Reid
Printer: Mazer

For permission to use material from this text, contact us:
web   www.thomsonrights.com
fax   1-800-730-2215
phone   1-800-730-2214

Printed in the United States of America
4 5 6 7 8 9 10

Wadsworth Publishing Company
10 Davis Drive
Belmont, CA 94002

International Thomson Publishing Europe
Berkshire House
168-173 High Holborn
London, WC1V 7AA, United Kingdom

Nelson ITP, Australia
102 Dodds Street
South Melbourne
Victoria 3205 Australia

Nelson Canada
1120 Birchmount Road
Scarborough, Ontario
Canada M1K 5G4

International Thomson Editores
Seneca, 53
Colonia Polanco
11560 México D.F. México

International Thomson Publishing Asia
60 Albert Street #15-01
Albert Complex
Singapore 189969

International Thomson Publishing Japan
Hirakawa-cho Kyowa Building, 3F
2-2-1 Hirakawa-cho, Chiyoda-ku
Tokyo 102, Japan

International Thomson Publishing Southern Africa
Building 18, Constantia Square
138 Sixteenth Road, P.O. Box 2459
Halfway House, 1685 South Africa

ISBN 0-534-36324-5

CONTENTS

INTRODUCTION

This Student Workbook is designed to accompany the video *Evolution of a Group,* published by Brooks/Cole • Wadsworth. The video and workbook are an interactive self-study program to be used for self-study with group counseling textbooks. The video and the workbook emphasize the application of concepts and techniques appropriate to the various stages of a group's development. The workbook requires that you become an active learner in your study of group process in action.

Key features of the workbook are:

- A pre-viewing self-inventory
- A group leadership skills checklist
- Process commentaries which address facilitation of the group process and interventions made with individuals
- A summary of member functions, leaders functions and key themes for each of the four group stages
- A strategy for drawing on a variety of techniques
- Questions to consider in understanding group process
- Questions to consider as the leaders assist members doing their work
- Exercises and activities for you to complete
- A commentary on group process developments and issues surrounding the work done by individual members
- A follow-up self-inventory at the end of the program
- A list of references for further reading

Evolution of a Group is a new concept in the training of group leaders. This two-hour educational video is designed to bring to life the development of a group at a three-day residential workshop co-facilitated by Ms. Marianne Schneider Corey and Dr. Gerald Corey. The group workshop included people who were real group members willing to explore their own issues and concerns. They were neither actors following a script nor were they role-playing the topics.

SYNOPSIS OF VIDEO

Evolution of a Group is a compilation of the significant group process and leadership techniques that occurred over a three-day residential group therapy session. You will see the development of the group process and how the leaders facilitated that process as the group moved through the four stages: initial, transition, working, and ending.

In the initial stage, the focus is on building trust and focusing on the here-and-now. The leaders set the stage by exploring ground rules for the group operation and assisting members in developing goals for the three days. In the transition stage, identifying and challenging member fears, hesitations, and resistance are the main topics. The level of trust is deepening and members begin reluctantly to talk about personal material.

The working stage is characterized by a high level of trust, clearer goals, and members exploring feelings, ideas and beliefs. The leaders help members explore their issues by focusing on the here-and-now so that members are not just "talking about" their issues, but actually experiencing them. Group cohesiveness is high and members interact with each other with less reliance on the leaders. In the ending stage, the group members review what they have learned, discussing how they will actually put those learnings into action, and prepare for ending the group.

Throughout the video you will see us, Marianne and Jerry Corey, co-leading and facilitating the group process. We utilize a variety of group techniques from various group treatment approaches. We strive to facilitate the mutual trust and support of the members, challenge them when needed, and at times, use humor therapeutically. It is the combination of viewing both the implementation of group leadership techniques and the movement of the group through the four stages of group process that makes this a unique video training program.

LEARNING OBJECTIVES

After viewing the video and completing the Student Workbook that accompanies this video, you will be better able to:

1. identify the major characteristics of each of the stages of a group.
2. apply certain techniques in opening and closing a group session.
3. discuss the importance of focusing on the here-and-now interactions within a group.
4. understand how past experiences can be worked with in the present.
5. discuss the value of self-awareness in knowing your values and how they affect you as a group counselor.
6. identify the major tasks of group leadership at each of the stages of a group.
7. identify the major functions and roles of co-leaders.
8. identify the roles and expectations of group members at the various stages of a group.
9. discuss how group leaders can effectively work with issues of cultural diversity in a group.
10. discuss the importance of building a climate of trust in a group setting.
11. discuss ways to formulate an agenda for a group session.
12. apply specific skills that help members formulate personal goals in a group.

RESOURCE TEXTBOOKS

This Student Workbook is designed to provide a self-study guide for you and accompanies the video. The Student Workbook is also designed as a supplement to several of the Coreys' textbooks in group counseling, and is designed to be used as a combined package of video, workbook, and textbook. The video and workbook can also be effectively coupled with other standard group counseling textbooks, some of which are listed in the annotated reading list.

We'll be making frequent reference to three of our texts that we have co-authored, as these are ideal companions to your self-study video and this workbook, which are:

Theory and Practice of Group Counseling (5th Edition, 2000) (And *Student Manual for Theory and Practice of Group Counseling*). (By Gerald Corey; published by Brooks/Cole • Wadsworth).

Groups: Process and Practice (5th Edition, 1997) (Co-authored by Marianne Schneider Corey and Gerald Corey; published by Brooks/Cole).

Group Techniques (2nd Edition, 1992) (Co-authored by Gerald Corey, Marianne Schneider Corey, Patrick Callanan, and J. Michael Russell; published by Brooks/Cole).

WELCOME TO THE SELF-STUDY PROGRAM

As you view the video we hope you do so with an openness to learn about how group process works—and with a willingness to examine your own beliefs as a group leader. This program can provide the experiential piece that helps you more concretely understand the nature of group process, and it can be a catalyst that prompts you into self-exploration. Your ability to function effectively as a group leader has a great deal to do with the degree to which you possess self-awareness and are willing to draw upon your personal resources in facilitating others in understanding themselves. The art of group leadership is far more than a technical endeavor; it involves your capacity to use your intuition and human responses. To be sure, effective group leaders need a theoretical grasp of group process along with the knowledge and skill base to make effective interventions in a group. Competent group leaders possess self-understanding, knowledge of dynamics of behavior and group process, and technical skills in group facilitation.

In teaching courses in group counseling or training group leaders, we often ask students to participate in a group demonstration. We typically have students participate in a group session and work with some of their real concerns. We find that this experiential learning contributes to a deeper understanding and appreciation of group work in actual practice. Through their own participation in a group experience, they are able to recognize their countertransference and unfinished business that could impede their therapeutic work with clients. It seems much more meaningful to students to talk about matters such as trust building, confrontation, providing feedback, working with resistance, and working in the here-and-now—as they actually experience each of these in a group situation—rather than exclusively relying upon learning about group process from readings and lectures. We hope that the combination of this video, workbook, and group counseling textbook supplies the experiential dimension required to give you a more realistic picture of the power inherent in a cohesive group.

HOW TO MAKE BEST USE
OF THE VIDEO AND WORKBOOK

> **NOTE: This video is not designed to be a stand-alone program. It is essential that the video be utilized in conjunction with the Student Workbook in the context of a course or workshop along with a textbook on groups. Since the original 20 hours of the group process were edited down to less than two hours, viewers have access to the Student Workbook that provides a context for those portions of the group not seen in the video.**

The purpose of this self-study video is to provide you with an opportunity to observe how a real group in action evolves from the beginning to the end. The aim of the video is to raise questions and issues, and to help you understand the art of facilitating a group. We do this by demonstrating how the various stages of a group, which we describe in our group texts, are played out with a group.

This video is a major visual tool that presents a demonstration of the evolution of a group. Although the group consisted of about 20 hours of actual working time, you will see less than two hours of condensed material taken from the group. The workbook supplies some process commentary on material taken from the actual group that you may not see in the video. We hope you will use the workbook as your "interpreter" of the group process. In the workbook we provide a rationale for the interventions we have made, discuss where an individual's work moved beyond that which is shown in the video, and involve you in what you are viewing by providing questions in the workbook.

Of course, reading about topics such as the stages of a group's development and other group process concepts will be an essential part of your self-study program. Refer to the textbook for discussion of each topic raised in video, and do the text reading either before or after you have viewed a particular segment. Then go through the workbook that accompanies this video and complete the activities. Actively engaging in this interactive process will ensure that your learning about group process is more vivid and personally meaningful.

We have a few suggestions on how best to view and work with the video. Watch the entire video without interruption once to get the sense of the general unfolding of the group. Then, watch the video in segments. Stop at each pause point in the video which is identified by an icon with the stage and number that corresponds to sections in the workbook. For each segment of work, or for each main interaction within the group, we have a series of questions to challenge your thinking on the situation you are seeing.

Complete as many of the exercises and activities as possible in the workbook, which walks you step-by-step through this self-study video. Before each of the *Stages of Group Development* sections, we have a self-inventory that we suggest you take. The inventories will help you focus on the issues to be explored and assist you in identifying your viewpoints on a range of topics as they apply to member issues, leader issues, and key tasks to be accomplished at each stage in a group's development. You'll find questions for each of the sections, as well as places to write your responses. The blanks provided for you to write your responses will result in you personalizing and co-authoring this workbook.

How can you get the most from this video? As you watch the video, we hope you become an active learner. Imagine that you are a group member when you watch the video (once or several times). We recommend that you replay each segment of the program several times to gain a clearer picture of the subtleties of leadership and group process. After viewing the video from the vantage point of a group member, put yourself into the situation as a group leader. As you study the video from the group leader's perspective, think of the leadership skills needed to effectively intervene and reflect on the way you might approach therapeutic work with individual members.

There are many icons indicating pause points that refer you to the workbook to help you assess and clarify your thinking, both as a member and as a leader. It is a good idea to routinely ask yourself the following questions after every segment of work within a stage of the group:

1. What do you imagine it would be like to be the group member in this particular situation? If you were the member, how much trust would you feel?
2. What issues come up for you as you watch a particular member work or observe interactions between members?
3. What reactions do you have to how the group leaders worked with each group member?
4. What are you learning about the use of group leadership skills and techniques from viewing a particular interaction?
5. What is the degree of trust you sense in the group?
6. How are the co-leaders working together?
7. What are you learning about applying group process concepts to an actual group from viewing specific segments of work?
8. How can you apply what you are viewing to working with different kinds of groups?

We have found that others who viewed this group were emotionally affected, since observing the work of the members triggered personal issues of the viewers. For instance, the video crew who participated in making this video were all very much moved by what they saw and heard during the weekend group. Even though they were professionals with a job to do, they also found themselves drawn into the genuine interactions that unfolded. We suspect that many of you will identify with some of the members of this group, as the themes explored in this group represent universal human struggles.

It is our position that group leaders bring to their professional work their life experiences and their personal characteristics. If you plan to lead groups, it is essential that you are aware of any potentially unresolved personal conflicts—and that you demonstrate a willingness to address these conflicts. Our assumption is that you will be able to facilitate a member's work to the degree that you have been willing to engage in your own journey into yourself. If you have led an unexamined life, it is not likely that you will have the resources to inspire others to challenge themselves to take the risks necessary to grow. For a more complete discussion of the personal characteristics of an effective group leader, refer to the discussion in: *Groups: Process and Practice* (Chapter 3); *Group Techniques* (Chapter 1); and *Theory and Practice of Group Counseling* (Chapter 2).

One way of getting more from the video for your own personal growth is to discuss your reactions with others. Certainly you can use the video and workbook for the purposes of your individual study. However, we highly recommend you form a small group to view and discuss selected points in the video. You can do this by getting a small study group together for the purpose of exchanging ideas, or you can do this by talking to another person who is in your class. If you are a student in a group counseling class, a small discussion group can be relatively easy to organize. The process of interaction in a small group can really increase the learning value of this program. Different individuals will bring different perspectives to what is being seen. Furthermore, various students and practitioners observing this group in action will most likely have many different ideas about ways to proceed with individual members and how to deal with interactions within the group. From our perspective, we do not want to communicate the belief that there is only one right intervention for each problem situation. In deciding how to make interventions in a group, leaders are influenced by what draws their interest, their theoretical orientation, their level of experience, and a host of other factors. Being in a small group will stimulate discussion of the many ways of pursuing therapeutic work in a group.

ACKNOWLEDGMENTS

We would like to thank the group members for participating in the development of this educational video on the evolution of a group. We admire them for their courage to be themselves and for their willingness to explore real concerns and issues. Their work in this project provided an opportunity for viewers to see a real group in action, rather than one that was scripted or role-played. The additional benefit of the group members' work is that many viewers may be touched in a way that serves as a catalyst to do their own work as well.

Thanks to the group members:

Andrew	Jacqueline
Casey	James
Darren	Jyl
Jackie	SusAnne

PRETEST AND POSTTEST: A SELF-ASSESSMENT

AN INVENTORY OF YOUR VIEWS ON THE PROCESS
AND PRACTICE OF GROUPS

The purpose of this inventory is to get you to think about a wide array of group techniques and related group process issues before you read about them in this Student Workbook and view them on the video. This inventory is designed to introduce you to some basic issues pertaining to group process and to the practice of group work as well, with special emphasis on these issues as they are relevant at the various stages in a group's life.

This is not a traditional multiple-choice test in which your task is to select the one best answer. Instead, the instrument is aimed at challenging you to reflect on your thoughts and attitudes about ways that you might work with the struggles and concerns of clients. For each item, circle the letter of the response that most clearly reflects your viewpoint at this time. In some cases you might want to circle more than one response. If you do not like any of the four responses listed you can write in your own response next to the letter "e", or you may use the blank line next to "e" to qualify your response.

After you have completed the video and workbook, we recommend that you retake this self-inventory by using it as a posttest. By taking this self-assessment, both at the beginning of the self-study program and then again at the end, you can assess any changes you have made regarding your attitudes about group process.

We recommend that you bring your inventory to class and use this as a basis for discussion of group process and group leadership techniques.

1. The major problem that I expect to face as a beginning group leader is:
    a. feeling devastated when I make a mistake.
    b. knowing which techniques to use at the appropriate time.
    c. being able to apply theory to practice.
    d. being able to effectively cope with resistant group members.
    e. _____

2. Of the following choices, I think the most important characteristic of an effective group leader is:
    a. goodwill and caring.
    b. courage.
    c. inventiveness.
    d. nondefensiveness in coping with attacks.
    e. _____

3. When I think about my own personal characteristics, I think that my strongest point is in my:
    a. openness.
    b. stamina.
    c. willingness to seek new experiences.
    d. sense of humor.
    e. _____

4. I would conceptualize my own theoretical orientation as a focus on:
    a. feeling.
    b. thinking.
    c. behaving.
    d. the integration of feeling, thinking, and behaving.
    e. _____

5. Of the following group-leadership skills, I would say my greatest strength is in:
    a. empathizing.
    b. interpreting.
    c. confronting.
    d. supporting.
    e. _____

6. Of the following group-leadership skills, I expect to encounter the most difficulty with:
    a. linking.
    b. blocking.
    c. terminating.
    d. reflecting.
    e. _____

7. In choosing a co-leader, a characteristic I would most look for is:
    a. a person who thinks just as I do.
    b. a person that I would like to be best friends with.
    c. a person that had a different theoretical orientation from mine.
    d. a person who would be willing to challenge me openly in the group.
    e. _____

8. What I consider to be the major advantage of the co-leadership model is:
    a. the fact that another person will share the leadership responsibility.
    b. the opportunity to process the group with another person.
    c. the opportunity for the members to see two of us with different styles in our way of working.
    d. having another person's perspective when conflicts occur within the group.
    e. _____

9. When I think about the possibility that my co-leader and I may not always agree, I think that I would be inclined to:
    a. want to discuss our differences openly in the group.
    b. never openly disagree in front of the other members.
    c. want to talk to my co-leader privately before airing our differences in the group.
    d. find another co-leader.
    e. _____

10. Of the following, the most pressing ethical issue I expect to encounter as a group worker is:
    a. knowing how to maintain confidentiality.
    b. providing for informed consent among the members.
    c. obtaining the necessary training for effective group leading.
    d. dealing with diversity within the group.
    e. _____

11. If I were unable to screen members on an individual basis for a group that I would be leading, the alternative that I would most likely use is:
    a. conduct a pre-group meeting for screening purposes.
    b. write a detailed letter to prospective members informing them about the group and my expectations.
    c. trust the members to decide for themselves if they were appropriate for my group.
    d. ask the members during the first few meetings to think about their readiness to become involved in this group.
    e. _____

12. If a member were to tell me during the screening interview, "I really don't want to be in this group, but I'm coming here because they sent me," I would be inclined to reply to this person:
    a. "If you don't want to be in this group, I don't want to accept you in here."
    b. "How does it feel to be sent here by someone else?"
    c. "What are your expectations of what this group will be like?"
    d. "I would like you to come for at least three sessions and give it a try and after that, we can decide if the group is of benefit to you."
    e. _____

13. During the initial stage of a group, what I think is my most important function as a group leader is:
    a. to model the behaviors that I hope the members will acquire.
    b. to teach members what group process is all about.
    c. to help members learn to deal with their feelings.
    d. to help members define their personal goals and the means for accomplishing them.
    e. _____

14. One of the most important group-process concepts at the initial stage is:
    a. teaching members group norms.
    b. helping the group to become a cohesive unit.
    c. teaching appropriate patterns of self-disclosure.
    d. creating an atmosphere of trust and safety.
    e. _____

15. Regarding the role of confrontation during the initial stage of a group, I would say that:
    a. confrontation will usually fragment the group at this stage.
    b. careful and caring confrontation will help develop trust and cohesion.
    c. confrontation can certainly lead to a group getting stuck.
    d. confrontation should be avoided at all costs during the first few meetings.
    e. _____

16. Regarding the matter of the degree of structuring that I would want to provide a group as a leader, I would say that:
    a. I would tend to be very structured during the beginning phase.
    b. I would be unstructured and allow the members to provide their own structure.
    c. this matter needs to be determined on the basis of the particular kind of group that I am leading.
    d. the group will flounder if I fail to provide structure throughout the duration of the life of a group.
    e. _____

17. If a member were to issue a clear challenge to me as a group leader by saying that I was not leading the group properly, I think my inclination would be to:
    a. ask this member to tell me more and attempt to listen nondefensively.
    b. challenge this member in return.
    c. interpret this challenge as a sign of transference and attempt to work with this transference in the group.
    d. ask other members if they agree or disagree with this member's challenge.
    e. _____

18. If two members seemed to be engaged in a conflict that was not getting resolved, my inclination would be to:
    a. ask the members to step outside and settle their differences alone before coming back to the group.
    b. see if I could bring other members into this conflict.
    c. tell the members how I am personally affected by their conflict.
    d. do anything I could to get past this conflict, since I know that I am uncomfortable with conflict.
    e. _____

19. If Randy, a group member, used hostility as a pattern in the group, I think my stance would be to:
    a. confront this member in a direct way about this behavior.
    b. ask the member if any of his behavior reminds him of the way he behaved as a child in his family.
    c. ask the members to give him feedback.
    d. ignore him and hope that he would eventually be quiet.
    e. _____

20. When members cry in a group, my general tendency is to:
    a. shift the focus quickly to someone else.
    b. ask them to talk about something positive.
    c. quickly offer support by reaching out with a touch.
    d. become silent and wait until they stop crying.
    e. _____

21. My thinking on the use of techniques in a group is to:
    a. use them when the energy is low and not much seems to be happening in the group.
    b. avoid using any preplanned technique or exercise, as doing so implies a lack of trust in the group members.
    c. use techniques that focus on what is happening in the here-and-now.
    d. encourage the members to come up with their own techniques.
    e. _____

22. Regarding the role of self-disclosure of the group leader, my view is that:
    a. I should be willing to expose my personal problems to the group.
    b. I should keep myself removed from the group so that I can be objective.
    c. I should express my persistent reactions to the members.
    d. I should always know my purpose for disclosing and ask myself how the disclosure will be therapeutic.
    e. _____

23. Of the following, the most important task during the final stage of a group is:
    a. dealing with feelings of separation.
    b. teaching members how to carry their learnings into real life.
    c. providing opportunities for practicing behavioral change.
    d. dealing with unfinished business.
    e. _____

24. In my view, the use of homework assignments as an adjunct to a group is:
    a. absolutely essential if members are to carry what they learn in the group to the outside world.
    b. useful if it is what a member wants.
    c. something that should be done collaboratively with a member.
    d. generally not too helpful.
    e. _____

25. My views on arranging for a follow-up group meeting could best be summarized by saying that:
    a. a follow-up meeting is essential for determining the long-range outcomes of a group.
    b. this is one way for members to avoid dealing with the ending of a group.
    c. such a meeting would be nice, but I see it as very impractical.
    d. this kind of meeting is very helpful for accountability purposes.
    e. _____

After completing this self-inventory early in this self-study program, look for any patterns in your responses. Once you've completed the video and workbook program, take the time to retake this inventory to determine if there are any changes in your thinking about the practice of group work.

GROUP LEADERSHIP SKILLS: A CHECKLIST

What follow are some questions you can use in applying the various leadership skills to specific pieces of work you will observe in the video. Throughout the video, attempt to identify specific group leadership skills that are being demonstrated by the co-leaders. At many of the icons, you can explore what skills you would need to intervene effectively. You can use these questions to reflect on your strengths and weaknesses as a group leader throughout this video.

1. **Active listening**
   a. How well are you able to listen to members?
   b. Are you sensitive to nonverbal messages?
   c. What sometimes gets in your way of listening to others?

2. **Reflecting**
   a. Are you able to reflect without becoming a hollow echo of another?
   b. Are you able to reflect accurately?
   c. Do your reflections help members explore more fully what they are feeling?

3. **Clarifying**
   a. Does your clarification help clients to sort out their feelings?
   b. Do members get a clearer sense of what they are thinking and feeling through your clarifications?
   c. Do your clarifications typically lead to increased member self-exploration?

4. **Summarizing**
   a. Are you able to identify common themes in a session?
   b. Can you help give direction through your summary remarks?
   c. Are you able to give an accurate summary, especially at the end of a session?

5. **Facilitating**
   a. Are you able to assist members in identifying and expressing whatever they are experiencing in the present?
   b. Do you foster interaction among the members?
   c. Are your interventions designed to increase the level of member responsibility for what happens in the group?

6. **Empathizing**
   a. Do your life experiences provide a basis for genuinely understanding the struggles of your members?
   b. Can you express your empathy to members so that they feel understood by you?
   c. Are you able to identify with others without getting overly involved and lost in their pain?

7. **Interpreting**
   a. Do you present your interpretations in such a manner that members are encouraged to think about what you say?
   b. How often are your interpretations appropriate and well-timed?
   c. To what degree do you encourage members to make their own interpretations?

8. **Questioning**
   a. Do you use open or closed questions more frequently?
   b. Do you keep yourself hidden by asking many questions?
   c. Do you ask "how" questions or "why" questions?

9. **Linking**
   a. Do your interventions foster member-to-member interactions or leader-to-member interactions?
   b. Do you value promoting an interactional focus in a group?
   c. How do you pay attention to cues that indicate common concerns?

10. **Confronting**
    a. To what degree do your confrontations invite people to look at themselves?
    b. What kind of modeling do you provide for effective confrontation?
    c. Are your confrontations related to specific behavior, rather than being global and judgmental?

11. **Supporting**
    a. To what degree do you provide positive reinforcement to members?
    b. Do you know when it is appropriate to offer support and when it is wise not to give support?
    c. Does your support result in members continuing a process of self-exploration, or does it lead to closure of an issue?

12. **Blocking**
    a. Are you aware of what behaviors to block in a group?
    b. Are you able to intervene effectively when a member is engaging in counterproductive behavior, or do you hold yourself back?
    c. Do you block firmly yet sensitively?

13. **Diagnosing**
    a. Can you make an assessment without labeling a person?
    b. Are you able to assess what a group needs at a given time?
    c. Do you know when a particular group might be counterproductive for an individual?

14. **Reality-testing**
    a. Do you help members to explore alternatives?
    b. Do you encourage members to test the reality base of their plans?
    c. To what degree do you teach members to apply what they learn in the group to their everyday lives?

15. **Evaluating**
    a. Do you teach members to continuously assess their level of participation in a group?
    b. Do you employ systematic means of evaluating a group?
    c. Do you spend some time openly discussing the progress of a group with the members?

16. **Terminating**
    a. Are you able to assist members in consolidating what they have learned in a group?
    b. Do you structure a group so that members are encouraged to transfer in-group learnings to situations outside of the group?
    c. Do you encourage members to continue working after they terminate a group?

PART 1 Forming a Group

COREYS' COMMENTARY: INTRODUCTION

About Forming This Group. This group is a closed and time-limited intensive group that met for about 20 working hours. Out of this, less than two hours of actual group interaction is shown in this videotape program. In this workbook, we base our teaching points both on what you will see in the video, and in some instances, on segments that were edited from the video due to time constraints. Part of this workbook is geared toward filling in the gaps of what was deleted. In particular we comment on group situations that assist us in making additional teaching points. We give an indication of how a particular situation developed, of how we continued working with members, and how they arrived at certain insights.

The group consisted of eight members (five women and three men) and two co-leaders. Although the group that was videotaped met as a residential group over three consecutive days, we want to emphasize that the process we describe (in both the video and in this workbook) does not differ a great deal from the process of a group that meets weekly. Certainly, the techniques we demonstrate could be used in groups that meet weekly and many of the concerns that the members raised are no different from personal issues that are typically explored in many therapy groups. Throughout this workbook, we ask how you might transfer what you are seeing in this video to the specific type of group or particular population with which you may work.

To provide some context for both the video and this workbook, it needs to be said that all the participants had some prior group experience. None of the participants were current students of ours; however, all of them did participate in a personal growth group co-led by us at different times. Very few of the participants in the video knew one another prior to agreeing to participate in this video. Most of them are in the helping professions and have at least a bachelor's degree in Human Services. One of them is in a doctoral program in Counseling. Two participants have a master's degree in Counseling, two are currently enrolled in a master's degree program in Counseling, and several will soon be going on for graduate study in the helping professions.

Pre-Group Meeting. It is ideal to arrange for a pre-group meeting after members have been screened and selected. This meeting is an orientation session where we provide further information regarding the group to help the members consider if this group is suitable for them. There were many special issues for these group members to consider regarding the filming and educational use of the material—issues of informed consent, confidentiality, revealing sensitive personal information, etc. If a pre-group meeting is impractical, then the first group meeting can be used to orient and prepare members for a successful group experience.

Before making the decision to be a part of this group, the members participated in a pre-group meeting in which they met with the co-leaders. At this time they had the opportunity to get acquainted with one another and determine whether they wanted to participate in this type of special group experience. Of course, all the participants knew in advance that the purpose of this workshop was to produce an educational video. We also discussed at length the special circumstances associated with participating in a group that is being videotaped. We wanted members to be themselves by sharing their real concerns, yet we emphasized it was for them to decide what specific personal subjects they would be willing to introduce. Furthermore, we reassured them that they had control over what would or would not be included in the final video. Throughout the weekend, they had opportunities to tell us if they wanted to omit any portion of their actual work. The members' veto power was pointed out to them at the pre-group meeting, during the weekend sessions, and after they returned home. We wanted them to have an opportunity to reflect on the work they did after the intensity of the weekend had subsided, and communicate any afterthoughts or reservations regarding the inclusion of some aspect of their participation in the final version of the video. Several members requested that we omit some of their disclosures, which we did. We thought this approach of respecting the members' decisions to edit out any of their work was far more preferable to being overly cautious during the group about moving into personal disclosures.

In the video you will first see the initial stage of the group which is a period of getting acquainted (or reacquainted), establishing group norms and ground rules, and beginning to develop a sense of trust. We assist group members in developing goals for their group work and identifying what might get in the way of accomplishing those goals. We directly address their hopes and expectations and also their fears and anxieties about the group. From early in the initial stage we focus members on the here-and-now.

Importance of Preliminary Preparation. Many groups that get stuck at some point do so because the foundations were poorly laid at the outset. What is labeled as "resistance" on the part of group members is often the result of the leader's failure to give them adequate orientation. This preparation can begin at the individual screening and can be continued during the initial session. Although building pre-group preparation into the design of a group takes considerable effort, the time involved pays dividends as the group evolves. Careful planning and preparation can avoid many potential barriers to a group's progress.

REFERENCES

For a more detailed discussion of issues pertaining to forming a group, see *Groups: Process and Practice* (Chapter 4). For a discussion of getting groups established and conducting a preliminary group session, see *Group Techniques* (Chapter 3, pages 34–40). For issues pertaining to forming a group, see *Theory and Practice of Group Counseling* (Chapter 4, textbook and student manual).

SUMMARY OF ISSUES IN FORMING A GROUP

The video did not actually show the selection process, the steps that were taken in getting ready for the video, the pre-group meeting that took place seven weeks before the filming, and all of the other important procedures leading to the formation of this group. However, we are including this summary of key issues pertaining to member functions and leader functions to give you a more complete picture of what led up to the actual first meeting that you see in the video.

Member Functions. Before joining a group, individuals need to have the knowledge necessary for making an informed decision concerning their participation. Members should be active in the process of deciding if a group is right for them. Following are some issues that pertain to the role of members at the formation stage:

- Members should know all the specifics about a group that might have an impact on them.
- Members can profit by preparing themselves for the upcoming group by thinking about what they want from the experience and identifying personal themes that will guide their work in a group.

Leader Functions. The main tasks of group leaders during the formation of a group include:

- identifying general goals and specific purposes of the group
- developing a clearly-written proposal for the formation of a group
- providing adequate information to prospective participants so they can make an informed decision
- conducting interviews for screening and orientation purposes

- selecting members, and dealing with members who are not selected
- organizing the practical details necessary to launch a successful group
- preparing psychologically for leadership tasks and meeting with co-leaders (if appropriate)
- arranging for a preliminary group session for the purposes of getting acquainted, presenting ground rules, and preparing the members for a successful group experience
- making provisions for informed consent and exploring with participants the potential risks involved in a group experience

QUESTIONS FOR DISCUSSION AND REFLECTION

1. In setting up a group, what are some of the major factors you would want to consider?
2. How would you go about recruiting, screening, and selecting members for one of your groups?
3. What do you think you need to do as a group leader to assist members in giving informed consent?
4. What kind of preparation would you want to provide to members of your groups? How might you orient them to the group experience?

PART 2 Initial Stage

SELF-INVENTORY TO COMPLETE BEFORE VIEWING THE INITIAL STAGE

Directions: Before each of the stages of the group you will see in the video, we have prepared a brief self-inventory. The purpose of the self-inventories is to help you identify and clarify your attitudes and beliefs about the variety of group process concepts, techniques, and issues in group leadership. Each of the statements on these inventories is not simply right or wrong, true or false. The point is to get you in an active frame of mind as you watch and reflect on the video and as you complete the workbook activities. Your task is to decide the degree to which you agree or disagree with these statements. Then, after reading the chapter, look over your responses to see whether you want to modify them in any way. These self-inventories will help you express your views and will prepare you to actively read and think about the ideas you'll encounter in this self-study program.

Using the following code, write next to each statement the number of the response that most closely reflects your viewpoint:

5 = I *strongly agree* with this statement.
4 = I *agree*, in most respects, with this statement.
3 = I am *undecided* in my opinion about this statement.
2 = I *disagree*, in most respects, with this statement.
1 = I *strongly disagree* with this statement.

_____ 1. I think that it is absolutely necessary to conduct a careful screening process for the groups I will lead.

_____ 2. I see my job as a group counselor to teach members what confidentiality is and how to best maintain it.

_____ 3. If at all possible, I would arrange for a pre-group meeting for orientation purposes.

_____ 4. In a well-conducted group, there are really no psychological risks for the group participants.

_____ 5. As a group leader, it is my job to establish ground rules for the participants.

_____ 6. Confidentiality is one of the most basic issues that needs to be addressed early in the course of a group.

_____ 7. A major function of leaders during the initial stage is to assist members in formulating concrete and personal goals.

_____ 8. To create a sense of trust among the members, I would be inclined to introduce a number of exercises in my groups.

_____ 9. As a way of creating an accepting climate, I'd engage in a fair degree of self-disclosure.

_____ 10. In general, there are more advantages than disadvantages to using a co-leadership model in a group.

The First Session. As you can see in the video, at the outset we ask the members to silently look around the room. Members typically make assumptions about others in the group, which we hope they will eventually check out to determine their validity. At this point, they are not asked to verbalize their reactions, but simply to note them. The purpose of asking people to look around the room and silently reflect is so that they can center themselves and get a sense of what they are thinking and feeling at the moment, especially their early reactions toward others. This will be useful material upon which we will draw at later sessions. At this early phase we make a concerted effort to teach participants how to pay attention to their own reactions and behavior in the context of what is occurring in the session.

We also make a bridge from the first time we met as a group, at the pre-group meeting. We ask them to say their names, mention any thoughts they have had since the pre-group meeting, and what it is like for them to come to this meeting. After they give their name, they are to repeat all the names of those who have spoken before them. By doing this everyone learns names and assures verbal participation from all members. An indirect outcome is that members typically speak up quickly, since they are concerned about remembering all the names.

The specific leadership skills that are especially important at this first session of the weekend group are: active listening, reflecting, clarifying, facilitating, and supporting. As you watch each segment of action on the video, refer back to the list of group leadership skills that are described earlier in this workbook. Identify which skills you think are most important at this time, and reflect on the degree to which you are able to apply each skill. Consider which skills represent your areas of strength and which skills need improvement.

REFERENCES

For a more detailed discussion of techniques for getting acquainted, focusing members, and teaching them how to pay attention to the group process, see *Group Techniques* (Chapter 4, pages 60–64). For a discussion of the survey of group leadership skills, see *Groups: Process and Practice* (Chapter 3); see also *Theory and Practice of Group Counseling* (Chapter 2, textbook and student manual).

QUESTIONS FOR DISCUSSION AND REFLECTION

At the various pause points in the video, we have supplied a process commentary explaining the reasons for our interventions or discussing member interactions or work. To assist you in becoming an active learner, we raise questions for you to consider, both as a group leader and as a group member. We suggest that you think about a particular kind of group that you may at some time design and lead. Think of a specific type of group and a specific age population. Apply the questions to a group you expect to lead. What modifications might you make? What cultural factors will you take into consideration? What skills might you apply to a particular situation? How would you implement the specific techniques we identify?

Taking the time to reflect on these questions and writing down your responses will assist you in learning practical applications. In deciding what to write as a leader response to different situations, we hope that you give yourself latitude by experimenting with a range of responses. We find that students freeze up when they are overly concerned about making mistakes and when they are too focused on saying and doing the "right" thing. The purpose of this workbook is to give you practice in clarifying your thinking and refining your responses. Rather than burden yourself with giving "right" or "wrong" responses, let yourself give more immediate responses to the situations you observe in the video group. As you review what you've written, you can always rethink your reasoning for an intervention.

In addition to thinking about these questions from the leader's perspective, also imagine yourself as a member of this video group and respond from that vantage point. It will be useful to compare your responses with fellow students in a small group or in a class.

1. What purpose do you see in asking members to spend a few minutes in silence as they look around the room? What would you ask members to do or say after this, if anything?

2. What kind of group are you most interested in designing and leading?

3. If you were to arrange a pre-group meeting for a group you are forming, what would you most want to accomplish at this preliminary meeting? What information would you want to know?

4. If you were a member in this group, what do you imagine it would be like for you to be in the room? What would be your concerns, fears, hopes, and expectations?

5. As a group member, what information would you want to know?

INTRODUCING THE GROUP MEMBERS

Below is a list of the group members and a brief sketch of each in terms of what they say about themselves early in the group and what they might want to explore during the weekend.

- Jacqueline (late 40s) sometimes does not feel a part of various groups in which she is involved. She refers to herself as an African-American woman, who at times finds it difficult to relate to others and states that she often feels "marginalized." One of her goals is to explore ways in which she seeks approval from others.

- SusAnne (age 27), of Hispanic background, would like to explore relationships in her life. She wants to explore the price she is paying for staying safe and not taking the risks of pursuing the relationships she wants.

- Jyl (age 39), a Euro-American, is willing to deal with struggles pertaining to perfectionism, dealing with losses, and career aspirations. Jyl experiences difficulty in asking others for what she wants, or in letting others care for her.

- James (age 35) describes himself as an educated Chicano who feels that he has to "prove himself." Because of his cultural background, he often feels oppressed in certain situations.

- Andrew (age 35), a Euro-American, is struggling with deciding how close he wants to get to people, especially women. Having gone through a painful divorce, he is very protective of letting himself get involved in an intimate relationship again.

- Darren (age 27), of Hispanic background, sometimes worries about how he expresses himself and is concerned about the impression he makes. He sometimes feels young and it is difficult for him to fit in with a group. He realizes that he wants to feel a sense of belonging.

- Casey (age 23) refers to herself as a Vietnamese American. She struggles with messages that she received as a child, which now get in her way. She would like to challenge her fears of feeling judged that hold her back at times.

- Jackie (age 43), a Euro-American, puts a lot of pressure on herself to be perfect, to get everyone to like her, and to keep everyone happy. She sometimes feels that she is not good enough, no matter what she accomplishes.

Setting Goals. One of the main tasks during the initial stage is for the leader to assist members in identifying clear and specific goals that will influence their participation. For group sessions to have direction, it is essential that members clarify what they want from a group. This process of setting goals is important both at the beginning of a new group and at the start of each group meeting. Too often members come up with fuzzy and global goals; in this case, the leader's task is to help members translate vague goals into clear and workable goals. Furthermore, it is crucial that members establish goals that have personal meaning for them, as opposed to setting goals that others think are important for them to pursue. Members who are working on their own goals are more motivated than those who are talking about a particular behavior they think they *should* change.

1. If you were a member of this video group, what main goal would you identify as something you would want to explore?

_____

_____

_____

2. Refer to the list of group leadership skills. What specific skills do you think are most important in assisting members to formulate clear personal goals?

_____

_____

_____

3. Consider a group you may someday want to lead. How will you assist members in establishing concrete goals if they state what they want in vague terms?

_____

_____

_____

REFERENCES

For a more detailed discussion of ways to identify and clarify group member goals, see *Groups: Process and Practice* (Chapter 5). See also *Group Techniques* (Chapter 3, pages 41–42). See also *Theory and Practice of Group Counseling* (Chapter 4, textbook and student manual).

NOTE: Now watch the video until the first icon (similar to the one below) appears. Then stop and read this section. Do the same for each section marked with an icon.

1

Initial Stage

Early Developments and Interactions

From the outset we ask members to briefly report some things they've been thinking about since the pre-group meeting and what they are aware of at this moment as they are convening for this weekend group. James says he often feels like an outsider in his life. As we listen to James, our interest is in finding out how James perceives himself in this group. We ask him, "Do you feel like an outsider in here?" We hope he will verbalize what it is like to be an outsider both in and out of group.

Jacqueline reports that she feels stupid and thinks that she rambles and makes no sense. It is important to find out what feeling stupid and being inarticulate mean to her. We do not assume that we know what she means by rambling. Our interest is in finding out if and how this is problematic for her. We might make the assumption that she has a critical judge within her; we do not pursue this at this point. Instead, we ask her to mention a few ways that feeling stupid gets in the way of what she wants.

Andrew acknowledges that, like James, he too feels like an outsider. When Marianne inquires whether he feels like an outsider with everyone in this group and whether there are some with whom he can make a connection, he tells us that he finds it is easier to trust the men in the group. The inquiry is aimed at getting Andrew to note that he does not feel equally distant from everyone. Again, we do not assume that we know what being an outsider means to Andrew or James, nor do we know what feeling stupid is like for Jacqueline, so we ask all three of them to note and verbalize when they become aware of these feelings.

As you look at this segment of action in the video, consider the following questions and your response to them.

1. Can you identify with any of the statements made by James, Jacqueline, or Andrew? If so, what are they?

_____

_____

_____

2. James says, "I feel like an outsider." What might you say to him?

_____

_____

_____

3. Jacqueline says, "I feel stupid when I ramble." What might you say or do if she became critical of herself at the first session?

_____

4. What purpose do you see in asking members to state verbally what they have been thinking or feeling before a session?

_____

_____

_____

5. What group leadership skills are especially important at this time?

_____

_____

_____

2

Initial Stage

Some Teaching About Group

We know that confidentiality is essential if members are to feel a sense of safety in a group and is basic for them to engage in risk taking. Even if nobody raises this issue, we raise the topic and caution them about how it can be broken. We then provide guidelines for maintaining the confidential nature of the exchanges. Specifically, we emphasize how easy it might be to break confidentiality without intending to do so. We ask them to refrain from talking about what others are doing in the group. We emphasize to members that it is their responsibility to continually make the room safe by addressing their concerns regarding how their disclosures will be treated. If they do not feel trust because they are afraid that others will talk outside the group, this doubt will certainly hamper their ability to fully participate.

We also mention to members that it does not make sense to open up too quickly without a foundation of trust. As is evident in the video, the way to create trust is to get members to verbalize their fears, concerns, and here-and-now reactions during the early sessions. We emphasize that it is up to each member to decide what to talk about and how far to pursue a topic. During the early phase of a group, we are not likely to make interventions that lead to in-depth exploration of what members are saying. Rather than focusing immediately on the first member who speaks, we make sure that everybody has a chance to briefly introduce himself or herself.

1. You are meeting your group for the first session. What would you most want to tell them about confidentiality?

_____

_____

_____

2. Specifically, what would you do to facilitate the development of trust at the first meeting of a group you were leading?

_____

_____

_____

3. Imagine yourself as a member at the first meeting. What fears do you think you might have about participating? What would help you to feel more trusting?

_____

_____

_____

REFERENCES

For a discussion of techniques for creating trust, see *Group Techniques* (Chapter 4, pages 65–69). For a discussion of specific attitudes and actions leading to trust, see *Groups: Process and Practice* (Chapter 5). For a discussion of factors to consider during the early phases of groups, see *Theory and Practice of Group Counseling* (Chapter 4, textbook and student manual).

```
┌─────────┐
│    3    │
│         │
│ Initial │
│  Stage  │
└─────────┘
```

The Dyad Exercise

Marianne gives instructions to members about how to make best use of the group, and then introduces a dyad exercise. Working in pairs facilitates member interaction, since talking to one person seems less threatening than addressing the entire group. We ask members to say a few things to their partners that they have been thinking about since we first met at the pre-group meeting. Specifically, we suggest they talk about any fears or expectations they have about this group, and anything they hope to explore in the group. We typically have them talk for about ten minutes to a partner and give them a chance to participate in a couple of dyads. After the dyads, we ask members to take turns verbalizing to the entire group a few of the points they shared with the partner(s) in this exercise. Again, our aim is to hear from everyone, to clarify what they are saying, and to help them become more specific about their goals for the group. We avoid interventions that would facilitate deeper exploration for any of the members because we want ample time for all members to at least identify their concerns. While it may be tempting to stay with any one member for a great deal of time to work on what he or she initially brings up, we do not do so because it would be at the expense of including others. If all participants speak early on, it provides everyone with a better sense of each other. They usually discover some commonalities enabling them to identify with one another, which leads to a climate of trust.

1. What purpose do you see in using dyads at the initial session of a group you are leading? How would you apply the dyad exercise if your group were composed of: children? adolescents? elderly people? court-mandated clients?

_____

2. What other ideas do you have about ways to begin at the first group session? How would you promote interaction?

_____

_____

_____

REFERENCE

For a more detailed discussion of using dyads, see *Group Techniques* (Chapter 4, pages 62–63).

OUR GOALS AND EXPECTATIONS FOR THE BEGINNING OF A GROUP

In this section, we describe some specific norms we are actively attempting to shape during the first few group sessions and some relevant examples from the video. We make the assumption that participants will get the most from a group experience if they are taught how to best involve themselves in active ways during the sessions.

Full Participation

We expect everybody to become a participating member. If members do not bring themselves in spontaneously, we continue to invite them to speak. We are likely to say any of the following: "Let's hear from everybody. A few of you have not yet spoken. Even though it is difficult to speak up, we hope you challenge yourself to do so." Members may choose to share relatively little about events outside of the group, yet they can still actively participate by keeping themselves open to being affected by others in the group, and they can share this.

1. If you were a member of a group, what would help you to feel comfortable enough to speak about yourself?

_____

_____

_____

2. Assume that at the initial session a member in your group says to you, "I really don't have anything to say now, and I don't want to force myself to participate." As a leader, what would you say to him or her?

_____

_____

_____

3. As a leader, what would you say to a quiet member who tells you that in his or her culture it is considered impolite to speak up without being called upon to talk?

_____

_____

_____

REFERENCES

For a more detailed discussion of guidelines and suggestions for members, see *Group Techniques* (Chapter 4, pages 60–63). See also the section on helping members get the most from a group experience, and also the section on group norms at the initial stage, in *Groups: Process and Practice* (Chapter 5).

4
Initial Stage

Shared Responsibility

As leaders, we do not want to be the only ones working, nor do we want members to rely on us to consistently bring them into the interactions. A few examples from the video illustrate how we build a norm of shared responsibility. Marianne invites Jackie to bring herself into the group process after Jackie says, "If I bring myself in when someone else is talking, my fear is that I would interrupt what's going on." The co-leaders teach members how to best include themselves in what may be happening in the group at a given point. We tell members that they are not as likely to interfere with the group process if they share how they are affected at that moment by what is going on. Thus, we encourage Jackie to take the risk of possibly interrupting an interaction, rather than sitting in the group quietly while she waits for her turn to speak. Our attempt is to shape the norm for members to spontaneously enter into interactions when the current issue has meaning to them, rather than to rely on us to draw them in.

We teach members to take an active role in the process of monitoring what they are feeling, thinking, and doing. We do not want them to expect that we will know and point out when they are feeling scared, intimidated, or withdrawn. A few examples illustrate this point. James says he feels he has to prove himself. We want James to monitor specific times during the sessions when he becomes aware of striving to prove himself. We ask Jackie, who is aware of the authority figures (co-leaders) to pay attention to the times when the presence of Marianne and Jerry might get in her way of doing work. You will soon see Casey who says she fears being vulnerable and that she rehearses endlessly before finally speaking. We encourage her to speak up when she experiences feelings of vulnerability. Casey can accomplish this by simply announcing that she feels vulnerable and that she is rehearsing.

Casey is a good example of a member who is in the habit of censoring her expression of thoughts and feelings. She is afraid of being inappropriate or being judged if she voices what she is thinking. We encourage Casey to speak up, especially when she is having reactions to what is transpiring in the group. Hopefully, she will learn that this group is a safe place to discover what would happen if she more frequently says out loud what she is thinking and feeling.

Assume that you were co-leading this group. What would you say to each of these member's comments?

1. Jackie tells you, "I want you to call on me, because I am insecure about talking because I might interrupt others."

_____

_____

_____

2. James says, "I worry a lot that I need to prove myself to you all."

_____

_____

_____

3. Casey says, "I rehearse countless times before I speak because I want to say things right."

_____

_____

_____

4. If you were a member of this group and had made any of the above statements, what leader intervention would be helpful to you?

_____

_____

_____

5
Initial Stage

Role Plays

As you will notice throughout the video we frequently use role plays to have members show us how they struggle with a particular relationship rather than report stories about problematic relationships. We ask members to identify specific individuals in the group, who could represent significant others, and who could be helpful to them in furthering their work. Routinely, we instruct them not to talk about an issue, but to make it present by speaking directly to another person during a symbolic role play. Darren identifies people that could assist him as he explores his feelings of "being a young kid." He selects Andrew and James to be his older brothers and Jerry to be his father. By bringing a conflict into the present, we get a much better understanding of how Darren struggles with feeling young. Role-playing techniques facilitate a deeper understanding and insight, a greater emotional connection, and tend to draw others into the work by tapping into their own emotions. Engaging in a role play and symbolically reliving some painful experiences tends to help members release pent-up emotions and can be a catalyst for the beginning of a healing process. Experiential methods, such as role-playing, enable participants to attend to unfinished business from the past and allow them to find a different ending to a painful event. Members often are able to make a new decision about a particular life situation. When a conflict situation is enacted, members also have opportunities to practice more productive ways of relating to others.

Reflect on these questions from the vantage point of you being a group leader.

1. What purpose do you see in asking members to engage in role-playing, even at the early sessions?

_____

_____

_____

2. Assume you ask Darren to role-play and talk to his brother and he tells you, "I think role-playing is silly. I'd rather just tell you about my brother and how we just don't get along." What would you say to him?

_____

_____

_____

3. What would you say to a member who interrupts another member's role play by asking questions?

_____

_____

_____

4. Do you think role-playing techniques can be applied to different client populations? How are you likely to introduce a role play?

_____

_____

_____

5. What factors pertaining to a member's culture or gender might you consider before initiating a role play in this group?

_____

_____

_____

REFERENCE

For an in-depth discussion of role-playing techniques, see the Psychodrama chapter in *Theory and Practice of Group Counseling* (Chapter 8, Psychodrama).

Here-and-Now

We consistently ask members to pay attention to their present reactions to and perceptions about one another. For a group to achieve a genuine level of trust, it is essential that they express persistent reactions that pertain to what is going on in the context of the group. We underscore the importance of members saying what is on their mind, even though they fear that they may interrupt what is going on. When members keep their reservations to themselves, there is no way that we can deal with such concerns. When participants share certain reactions that could get in their way of participating fully in the group, we have a basis to do some productive work. For instance, Jackie lets us know that she will probably feel intimidated by us as authority figures, because she never feels good enough. She also shares that she tends to be cautious as a way to avoid hurting anyone's feelings or creating a conflict. With this information now being public, she is in a good position to use reactions that will emerge for her as a reference point for some intensive work.

We are interested in both a here-and-now focus and a there-and-then focus. However, we find that members are usually not ready to take the risk of dealing with significant personal issues outside the group until they first deal with their reactions to one another in the room. When members bring up either a present or past problem situation from outside of the group, we explore how this might be played out in the context of the present group. For example, James says that he often feels that he has to prove himself at work. Both Jacqueline and Jackie inform us how much they are seeking approval. Andrew talks about feeling isolated. All these members are asked to take note when they experience these feelings or thoughts in the group.

While we emphasize members' here-and-now reactions, we also ask them to explore how their present reactions in the group may reflect how they feel away from the group. Jackie expresses her concern that she will not live up to our expectations, nor will she get our approval. Eventually, as the group becomes more established, we hope that she will also increase her awareness of how her struggles operate in her everyday life.

1. As a *member*, how would you respond to a leader who emphasizes a here-and-now awareness? What difficulties might you expect in doing this?

_____

_____

_____

2. As a *leader*, what might you say or do to promote a here-and-now focus in your groups?

_____

_____

_____

6

Initial Stage

Making Contracts

As members state what they want to accomplish, we routinely ask them if they are willing to take the steps necessary to reach their goals. We also check to determine that the goals they are setting for themselves represent what they want, rather than goals they feel pressured to accept from someone else. Casey reports that she wants to rehearse and edit less, and express herself more often. She agrees to make a contract to more spontaneously express her inner thoughts. Marianne wonders if Casey's desire to challenge her own cultural injunctions is indeed her own agenda. She asks, "How come you want to change this?" Later in the group, Jerry suggests some work to Casey. When Casey hesitates, Marianne again asks Casey whether this is her agenda or Jerry's.

REFERENCE
For a more detailed discussion of preparing contracts, see *Group Techniques* (Chapter 3, page 42).

1. If you were a member of this group, how open would you be in agreeing to making a contract? What would help you in making a contract?

    _____

    _____

    _____

2. How, if at all, would you use contracts with a group you might lead? How would you help members design a contract?

    _____

    _____

    _____

```
┌─────────────┐
│     7       │
│             │
│  Initial    │
│  Stage      │
└─────────────┘
```

Direct Talk
Rather than have members talk *about* a concern they mention, we consistently ask them to select someone in the group to talk with directly. Also members have a tendency to talk about an individual in the group. When this occurs we instruct them to look at and talk directly to that person. For example, Jyl reveals that she is feeling very exposed. Marianne makes the assumption that when people feel exposed they are usually aware of someone noticing them, and thus, she inquires, "Whom do you notice?" After Jyl indicates that James is the one she notices, she is asked to look at James, speak directly to him and tell him what she is experiencing.

1. If you were a *member* in this group, how would you react if the leaders asked you to talk directly to another person?

    _____

    _____

    _____

2. If you were a *leader* in this group, what cultural factors might you consider before asking members to speak directly to one another?

_____

_____

_____

8
Initial Stage

Look and See

Throughout the duration of a group, we ask members to look at those with whom they are having reactions or making assumptions about. Jyl assumed that James was judging her; however, when she looked at him as she spoke to him, she began to see acceptance rather than judgment. Jyl would have missed that had she directed her eye contact away from James. With this we also help Jyl become aware of her projections. When Jacqueline indicates that she feels marginalized as an African-American woman and sometimes feels different around Euro-Americans, we ask her to look around the group and notice her reactions. We could have her address individuals by indicating some of the ways she feels different from them.

1. What do you think is the therapeutic value of asking members to look at another person in the group as they are talking about a problem area?

_____

_____

_____

2. What cultural variables might you consider in requesting a member to look at others?

_____

_____

_____

Avoiding Solutions

Rather than providing quick solutions, it is essential that members have an opportunity to express their feelings and thoughts. When a member raises self-doubts, fears, or struggles, we block other members from offering reassurance too quickly, before this individual has had an opportunity to explore his or her concern. When Jyl is crying as she is talking to James, we do not facilitate members giving her reassurance or telling her that she has no reason to feel embarrassed. Instead, when Jyl says she feels exposed, our intervention leads her to say more about what it is like for her to feel exposed. Although quick reassuring feedback from members may make her feel good for a brief moment, it is doubtful that this feeling will be long-lasting. This is based on the assumption that Jyl's critic lies within her and not primarily with others.

1. As Jyl is crying and saying she feels exposed, what do you, as a leader, imagine you would be thinking or feeling? What would you do?

_____

_____

_____

2. If you were leading this group, what are you likely to say to a member who asks Jyl many questions about why she feels embarrassed?

_____

_____

_____

9

Initial Stage

Dealing With Conflict

A group cannot achieve a genuine level of safety if conflict is brewing and is not addressed. Conflict may occur at any stage of a group. During the first session in this group, there was conflict between Jyl and James when she announced that she felt judged by him. Jyl's feelings were hurt when Jacqueline made the comment, "What I have to say is not very nice." Although Jyl did not let Jacqueline know how she was affected by her comment, it was crucial that the leader drew attention to Jacqueline's comment. Marianne, operating on her hunch that Jacqueline's comment did not register well with Jyl, asked Jyl what it was like to hear the remark. Jyl responded with, "Being me with you is not safe. I'm going to have to protect myself. The look on your face lets me know that I'm likely to be judged by you." Because both of them continued talking, they were able to resolve the conflict, and they were able to again establish trust between them.

The same was true for Jyl and James. Another potential conflict situation was prevented when Jyl gave her reactions to both James and Jacqueline when they were talking about not being taken seriously because of their ethnicity. Jyl admits that she does not know what it's like to be an African-American woman or an educated Chicano, yet she discloses how she struggles in a similar way when she says, "I know what it's like to be a white woman—an educated, white woman—who is sometimes treated like a piece of fluff." These examples show that conflict does not have to be divisive, if all who are involved express their reactions and continue the dialogue. What is crucial is that the leaders are alert to subtle conflict that may be brewing and teach members how to deal with one another. Leaders should not collude with members to avoid conflict; instead, they need to model that it is safe to address an interpersonal conflict, and that the conflict can be productively resolved. During the early stages of a group, the members are keenly aware of ways that conflict is being dealt with by the leaders and between members. If conflict is not addressed adequately, it is likely to have a significant impact on the trust and cohesion of the group at a later phase of development.

Reflect on these questions from the vantage point of being a leader of this group.

1. What do you say to Jacqueline when she makes the comment, "What I have to say would not be nice."

_____

_____

_____

2. What are you likely to do if you sense a conflict is brewing in the group, yet members deny that there is any tension?

_____

_____

_____

3. How well do you deal with conflict in your own relationships? How might your attitudes or fears about conflict either help or hinder you as a leader in dealing with conflicts in groups?

_____

_____

_____

4. What would you do if a conflict emerged with your co-leader at the early stage of a group?

_____

_____

_____

10
Initial Stage

What Will Get in Your Way in this Group?

We teach members to speak up, even if they have not yet formulated exactly what they want to say. We often say, "It is easy to let an entire session go by without getting around to bringing yourself into the group. The longer you wait to involve yourself, the more difficult it will become. Challenge yourself to say something at the beginning of each group, even if it's a brief statement of what it is like for you to come to group today." Members often discover that if they force themselves to express even briefly something that is on their mind as they come to a session, this will pave the way for them to become more involved. It is especially useful for members to monitor their internal dialogue and any hesitations they may have about participation and vocalize this.

Early in the course of a group we typically ask participants to reflect on what they are likely to do that will interfere with what they want from the group experience. We say something like, "What will you do when you become anxious? How might you resist? How could you sabotage yourself? What are you willing to do when you recognize that you are getting in your own way?" As co-leaders, we are not willing to assume responsibility for them to continually call them on their avoidances. Instead, we expect them to monitor what they are doing and call themselves on self-defeating behavior during the group.

When we asked members in the group to reflect on the questions listed in the previous paragraph, they readily identified some ways they could avoid when they got scared. Below are some examples:

Andrew: "I'll edit myself by trivializing. I tell myself that what I have to say is not that important. I'll let others talk and convince myself that they have more significant issues."

Casey: "I rehearse. I'm afraid I can't articulate my thoughts well enough for you to understand me. I want to sound intelligent. Because I think I have to be perfect, I may not let you know what I'm thinking."

Jacqueline: "I'm afraid I won't say things well. I beat myself up after a group. I tell myself that I didn't say what I wanted clearly enough."

Jackie: "I try hard not to react. I realize that when I'm hurt, but it is hard to say 'ouch.' "

Darren: "I feel young and invisible. I don't know how to get in with you guys, so I'm likely to withdraw."

James: "You won't know when I feel outside the group, because I won't tell you. I hold back."

Jyl: "When I get scared or feel like I'm being judged, I'll retreat."

SusAnne: "I'm afraid my problem will be so big that I won't be able to handle it. My first instinct is to disappear."

During the initial phase of a group, members typically appear somewhat hesitant to get involved. For example, we don't view SusAnne's statement above as mere resistance. Her hesitation may be related to a lack of trust in the leaders or the members to be able to handle a problem that she brings forth. Members may be intimidated by the leaders or certain other members, and they are sizing up one another. Some initial hesitation can be expected. What is important is how any early signs of resistance is dealt with by the leaders. Because we recognize that members are anxious, and that this anxiety can be used therapeutically, we begin by encouraging the members to share and explore their reactions.

As co-leaders, what we are likely to say to these members collectively is something like the following: "When you become anxious in this group, you are likely to behave exactly as you just described. I hope you call yourself on your behavior when you notice that you are avoiding. I may or may not notice it, so I need your help. When you get scared and withdrawn, push yourself to announce your reactions. Doing so will allow us to work together and give you an opportunity to do something different. Note what might happen if you behave in new ways when you find yourself becoming anxious."

1. Consider that you are co-leading this group. Pick one of the member's statements above and write your response to him or her.

_____

_____

_____

2. How are you likely to handle possible signs of resistance or hesitations you notice during a first session?

_____

_____

_____

3. How can you differentiate between hesitation that may be due to cultural background and resistive behaviors on a member's part?

_____

_____

_____

4. Assume you are a *member* of this group. What would you say about yourself regarding how you might hinder yourself from getting what you want out of the group? What would help you to challenge yourself?

_____

_____

_____

5. As a member, what would make you most anxious during an early session? How are you likely to deal with your anxiety?

_____

_____

_____

6. Review the list of group leadership skills in this workbook provided on pages 10–12. Which skills are especially pertinent in assisting members to deal with anxiety and avoidances on their part?

_____

_____

_____

A Co-Leadership Style

By this time, you have noticed our style of interacting with each other, and with the members, as co-leaders. We value co-leading, as it affords many opportunities for modeling the points we want to teach group members. The participants will learn more from how we actually behave in group sessions than by what we tell them. We suggest that you look for specific lessons that can be drawn from what you see of our co-facilitation style. As much as possible, we strive to be natural and spontaneous in our joint work. We do not decide beforehand who will say what or who will make what intervention. As you will notice, we frequently play off one another. In fact, there are times when we may have different ideas about how to pursue work with an individual member or different perceptions about initiating work in the group as a whole. At these times we simply talk out loud about our perceptions. From our vantage point, it is essential that you have a basic respect for, and trust in, your co-leader. You can have different styles of leadership, and these differences can even enhance your work together. What is important is that you make time to meet with your co-leader and to talk about your leading together.

1. What are some specific things you are noticing about the way the co-leaders work as a team?
2. What are some differences in style between Marianne and Jerry?
3. What is the most important thing you are learning about co-leadership from viewing the video?
4. What qualities would you look for in your co-leader?

5. What advantages do you see in working with a co-leader?

6. What potential disadvantages might there be in working with a co-leader?

REFERENCES

For a more detailed discussion of the co-leadership model, see *Groups: Process and Practice* (Chapter 3), with attention to the advantages and disadvantages of co-leading. For ideas of possible lines group leaders can use at the various stages of a group, see *Student Manual for Theory and Practice of Group Counseling* (Chapters 4 and 5). Chapter 2 of the manual contains guidelines for meeting with your co-leader. As a basis for discussion with your co-leader, you might want to use the self-evaluation of group-leader skills in Chapter 2 of the manual. In *Theory and Practice of Group Counseling* (Chapter 2) there is a section on co-leading groups.

COREYS' COMMENTARY: THE INITIAL STAGE

The initial phase of the group is a time for members to get to know one another. It is difficult to build a climate of safety if members do not have a sense of one another. It is not our intention to have members immediately focus on exploring their deeper personal issues at the first meeting, but to heighten their awareness of the atmosphere in the room. This is a time for orientation, getting acquainted, learning how the group functions, developing the norms that will govern the group, exploring fears and expectations pertaining to the group, identifying personal goals, and determining if this group is a safe place. The manner in which the leader deals with the reactions of members determines the degree of trust that can be established in the group.

In these early sessions we are shaping up specific group norms (working in the here-and-now, talking directly to one another, expressing persistent reactions, dealing with expectations and fears, establishing personal goals, and so on). Our main attention is on establishing a foundation of trust. We do this by getting members to talk about afterthoughts, by teaching them how to pay attention to what they are experiencing in the here-and-now, noticing their reactions to others in the group, and verbalizing these reactions. Notice that we do considerable teaching about how the participants can most productively involve themselves in the ongoing group process.

SUMMARY OF INITIAL STAGE

Basic Characteristics of the Initial Stage. The early phase of a group is a time for orientation and determining the structure of the group. Some of the distinguishing events of this stage are as follows:

- Participants test the atmosphere and get acquainted.
- Members learn the norms and what is expected, learn how the group functions, and learn how to participate in a group.
- Risk taking is relatively low, and exploration is tentative.
- Group cohesion and trust are gradually established if members are willing to express what they are aware of in the here-and-now.
- Members are concerned with whether they are included or excluded, and they are beginning to define their place in the group.
- A central issue is safety and being assured of a supportive atmosphere.
- Members may look for direction and wonder what the group is about.

- Members are deciding whom they can trust, how much they will disclose, how safe the group is, whom they are drawn to and with whom they feel distant, and how much to get involved.
- Members are learning the basic attitudes of respect, empathy, acceptance, caring, and responding—all attitudes that facilitate trust building.

Member Functions. Early in the course of the group, some specific member roles and tasks are critical to the shaping of the group:

- taking active steps to create a trusting climate
- learning to express one's feelings and thoughts, especially as they pertain to here-and-now interactions in the room
- being willing to express fears, hopes, concerns, reservations, and expectations concerning the group
- being willing to make oneself known to others in the group
- being involved in the creation of group norms
- establishing individual goals that will govern group participation
- learning how groups work and how to best participate in the process

Leader Functions. The major tasks of group leaders during the orientation and exploration phase of a group are:

- teaching participants the basics of group process
- developing ground rules and setting norms
- assisting members in expressing their fears and expectations and working toward the development of trust
- modeling the facilitative dimensions of therapeutic behavior
- being open with the members and being psychologically present for them
- showing members that they have a responsibility for the direction and outcome of the group
- providing a degree of structuring that will neither increase member dependence nor promote excessive floundering
- helping members establish concrete personal goals
- dealing openly with members' concerns and questions
- teaching members basic interpersonal skills such as active listening and responding
- assessing the needs of the group and facilitating in such a way that these needs are met

REFERENCES

For a discussion of group characteristics at the initial stage, group process concepts, and leader functions at the initial stage, see *Groups: Process and Practice* (Chapter 5). For a discussion of characteristics of the initial stage and techniques appropriate for the initial stage, see *Group Techniques* (Chapter 4). For a summary of issues pertaining to the early stages of a group's development, see *Theory and Practice of Group Counseling* (Chapter 4, text and student manual). For a discussion of applying different theoretical perspectives in working with themes emerging from the video group, see *Theory and Practice of Group Counseling* (Chapter 17, text and student manual).

QUESTIONS ON APPLYING THE SUMMARY LIST

Now that you have watched this segment of the group during its initial stages, apply the summary list from the previous page to the following questions concerning the video group.

1. What are the *main characteristics* of this group at its early stage of development?

_____

_____

_____

2. What *member functions* do you see being illustrated? As you observe the members, what stands out most for you at this phase of the group?

_____

_____

_____

3. Which member (or members) stands out most for you in this segment, and why?

_____

_____

_____

4. What *leader functions* do you see being illustrated? What specific skills and interventions are the co-leaders using at this phase of the group?

_____

_____

_____

5. What are you learning about co-leading a group by observing Marianne and Jerry co-lead this group?

_____

_____

_____

6. What are you learning about how groups either function or malfunction at this point?

_____

_____

_____

Take time to think about a particular kind of group, composed of a specific client population, that you are interested in designing and leading. Answer the following questions from that vantage point.

1. What *specific characteristics* might you expect at the initial stage of the group's development?

_____

_____

_____

2. What *member functions* do you see as being most important at this initial stage?

_____

_____

_____

3. What *leader functions* would you identify as being most crucial at this initial stage?

_____

_____

_____

4. At this phase in your group, what are three group leadership skills you see as being especially important? Which of these skills are strong areas for you? Which skills need improvement?

_____

_____

_____

5. What are the *main challenges* you expect to face at this stage in your group's development?

_____

_____

_____

6. If you were co-leading, what would you most want to talk with your co-leader about at this point in your group's development?

_____

_____

_____

QUESTIONS FOR DISCUSSION AND REFLECTION

1. During the early phase of a group, what kinds of norms would you be most interested in introducing into a group?
2. What things would you most want to teach members about how to get the most from one of your groups? How might you best teach members to take full use of the group experience?
3. What are your thoughts on how to encourage members to assume a share of the responsibility for the direction a group takes? Do you have ideas of ways you might increase the chances that members will become active participants?

4. How comfortable do you think you would be in introducing role-playing activities in your groups?
5. What ideas do you have for promoting a trusting climate in groups you will be leading?
6. What kind of behaviors do you most want to model for the members of your groups?
7. What would you have learned about yourself had you been a member or a leader of a group such as this one?
8. What ethical issues can you raise concerning this segment of the group?

PART 3 Transition Stage

SELF-INVENTORY TO COMPLETE BEFORE VIEWING THE TRANSITION STAGE

Directions: The purpose of the self-inventory is to help you identify and clarify your attitudes and beliefs about the variety of group process concepts, techniques, and issues in group leadership. Each of the statements on the inventory is not simply right or wrong, true or false. The point is to get you in an active frame of mind as you watch and reflect on the video and as you complete the workbook activities. Your task is to decide the degree to which you agree or disagree with these statements. Then, after reading the chapter, look over your responses to see whether you want to modify them in any way. This self-inventory will help you express your views and will prepare you to actively read and think about the ideas you'll encounter in this section.

Using the following code, write next to each statement the number of the response that most closely reflects your viewpoint:

5 = I *strongly agree* with this statement.
4 = I *agree*, in most respects, with this statement.
3 = I am *undecided* in my opinion about this statement.
2 = I *disagree*, in most respects, with this statement.
1 = I *strongly disagree* with this statement.

____ 1. If a member displays resistance, or if there is resistance in the group, this is a sure sign that the group leader is doing something wrong.

____ 2. Conflict among members indicates that there is not an adequate degree of trust in the group.

____ 3. If conflict were to arise, I would use some techniques to shift the focus to something more constructive.

____ 4. If a member were to say, "I feel that people will judge me," my intervention would be to ask members to give this person immediate positive feedback as a way to offer the member reassurance.

____ 5. If members express that they have fears about participating, my inclination would be to suggest they are probably not ready for this group.

____ 6. If I were to disagree with what my co-leader did in a session, I certainly would never bring this matter up in the group itself.

____ 7. If members are resistant, I think they need to be confronted immediately so this won't become a pattern.

____ 8. I would confront members with care and respect, even if they are difficult and if they say things to me that are difficult to hear.

____ 9. I expect the groups I lead to be composed of members who may be hesitant and scared of interaction.

____ 10. I think that support needs to be balanced with challenge.

Building Safety

Safety is a factor throughout the duration of a group. Establishing trust becomes even more important before a member is ready to engage in some deeper work. This group had established some degree of trust, yet all members were not at the same level. For example, SusAnne initiates some exploration of ways that she protects herself from being hurt with a wall. At some point during this discussion, Jerry asks her, "Do you think we will care about you enough to listen to you as you talk about your hurt?" SusAnne hesitates and then lets us know that she has doubts about our interest in her. Because of this, we do not facilitate SusAnne's work she initiated, but our interventions are aimed at getting SusAnne to establish the level of safety in the room that will be necessary for her to pursue deeper self-exploration.

Another teaching point we want to make pertains to the metaphor of the *wall* that SusAnne mentions. Eventually, we may return to her metaphor for further exploration at a later session. There are many useful interventions we could make, and which intervention we choose has a great deal to do with the clues we pick up from SusAnne. She gives us a sense of what direction she wants to move, and then we build upon that. Depending on what emerges into SusAnne's awareness, we might move in a number of different directions as we work with the metaphor of her wall. Some of these interventions are:

- "Describe this wall for us. How high is it? How thick is it? Does it surround you? Are there any openings in your wall?"

- "Let yourself become this wall and talk to each of us individually about what it is like for you as the wall."

- "Talk to us about what this wall does for you in your life. How does it help you? What functions does it serve? How might your wall get in your way in life? How do you imagine life would be if you did not have this wall? Are you willing to take the wall down a bit in this group?"

We would not ask all of these questions, nor make all of these interventions. The above represents a sample of some of the ways we might assist SusAnne in exploring what her wall means to her and the potential price she is paying for keeping her wall. It is not up to anyone in the group to decide that she should tear down the wall, for that is her decision. Instead, we want to create a safe climate that will allow her to explore the meanings of her metaphor.

We want to underscore an important point. In our view, there is not one right way to intervene when members identify a problem area they want to explore. There are no perfect words and there is no such thing as a perfect intervention. Depending on your style of group leadership, your theoretical orientation, and your perception of the context of what is going on in the group, you are likely to intervene in any number of ways. There are many fruitful ways to pursue therapeutic work that a client initiates. What is important is that you have an understanding of what you want to accomplish, and that this is in harmony with what your client wants to achieve. Although you won't know the outcome of a therapeutic experiment before it unfolds, you should have a rationale for your interventions.

1. If SusAnne declared she wanted to take down the wall that she uses to protect herself from hurt, what assumptions are you likely to make about what this means?

2. What intervention would you make with SusAnne, and what would you most hope to accomplish with it?

_____

_____

_____

3. To what extent do you burden yourself with the expectation that you have to make the perfect intervention or say things perfectly to a member?

_____

_____

_____

4. What ideas do you have about ways that you can begin to trust your intuitions more and be willing to take action with members?

_____

_____

_____

REFERENCE

For another detailed example and discussion of techniques used to explore a member's theme, "I don't feel safe in here", see *Group Techniques* (Chapter 5, pages 101–103). Another illustration of working with a member's theme, "I feel the burdens of the world", is described in the same book (Chapter 6, pages 132–134).

12
Transition Stage

Linking the Work of Members

One of the unique advantages of group counseling is that clients can learn from one another. Although some individual work in a group is useful, it is a better utilization of time and resources to involve several members. In this area the leaders help the group to identify common themes emerging within the group interactions. We want to create the norm that members can take the initiative to link themselves with others and not rely exclusively on the leaders to join them with others. One way for co-leaders to link members is to pay attention to nonverbal reactions of members, as is seen in the video segment described below.

You will notice that Andrew has a dilemma of wanting to be safe versus reaching out to others. He wants to appear strong and is afraid that others will see him as being weak. During Andrew's work, Marianne notices that Jyl is tearing up. The co-leaders involve Jyl by asking her to tell Andrew how he affects her. Both Andrew and Jyl can be engaged in a therapeutic dialogue. It is not necessary to drop Andrew in order to include Jyl. This is an example of enhancing one member's work by including others into the therapeutic exchange. The skill of linking is essential to maximize the therapeutic power inherent in a group.

Earlier Andrew mentioned that Jerry reminds him of his dad. Andrew now shares that he is feeling very self-conscious around Jerry because he does not want to appear weak. Marianne asks Andrew to express his feelings directly to Jerry, which he does. Jerry discloses to Andrew that he was tearing up and says, "What a shame that you have to surround yourself with a huge wall." Jerry's response was nothing close to what Andrew feared he might be thinking about him.

The reactions Jyl and Jerry shared toward Andrew did not confirm his feared hypothesis that people would not respect him if he let his guard down. Instead, he felt acknowledged and supported, which provided him with reinforcement to reveal more of the side of himself that he has locked up inside of him.

Andrew's dilemma of staying locked up versus needing others is a catalyst for others. James is drawn into Andrew's exchange with Jyl and with Jerry. James says, "I can identify with you. It takes a lot for me to feel I always have to be strong. I'd like to be able to tell my brother and father that it is okay to be weak." With this connection, we could invite James to talk more to Andrew, telling him what it is like to have to be strong all the time. By working together, both Andrew and James can make a decision about wanting to continue to live their lives as they have, or if they want to modify some aspect. Another way we could facilitate interaction would be to have James talk to Andrew as his brother, telling him ways he would like their relationship to be different. The symbolic role-play that James would do with his brother could also be enlightening to Andrew.

From the examples described above, you can see how it is possible to bring several members into a piece of therapeutic work by linking the common struggles. Even though their stories may be different, they can be linked with the common pain they experience. Jyl, who was emotionally moved by Andrew's work and felt connected to him, later did an extensive piece of work with her own father. Even though we shift our attention from member to member, we avoid doing so at any member's expense. For instance, we notice Jyl crying and we ask her to tell Andrew, who was the focus of our attention, what she is experiencing. Linking her to Andrew makes it possible for us to attend to both individuals. If members are having emotional reactions to Andrew, more often than not, his struggle has some personal meaning to them. Both Jyl and James, in the process of telling Andrew how he affects them, are not distracting his exploration.

1. Both Andrew and James feel they need to be strong. As a leader, what assumptions would you make in your work with them?

    _____

    _____

    _____

2. If Andrew declared he was tired of feeling locked up and wanted to be different, how would you pursue work with him?

    _____

    _____

    _____

3. What outcome would you want to see if you were facilitating a role-playing situation involving Andrew and his symbolic father?

_____

_____

_____

4. As you are working with Andrew and James, you notice that Jyl begins to cry. What would you do at this point?

_____

_____

_____

5. As a group leader, what catches your interest in the scenario described involving James, Andrew, and Jyl?

_____

_____

_____

6. What advantages do you see in linking members' agendas as you pursue work in a group, rather than focusing on one member at a time?

_____

_____

_____

7. From what you have seen in the video so far, what other possibilities do you see for linking exploration of different members' issues?

_____

_____

_____

8. As you watch the above segment of work on the video, what leadership skills do you see the co-leaders using?

_____

_____

_____

"How Was the Day?"

With any type of group we are leading, we set aside some time when we ask members to say how the session was for them. Specifically, here are some areas we cover with this group: "How was the day for you? In what ways do you feel any different now than you did at the beginning of the day? Do you have any regrets about anything you did or said? How safe does the room feel to you now? What specifically do you want to bring up tomorrow?" At this juncture, we are interested in bringing closure to this session and getting them focused on how they can involve themselves in the upcoming session. Here are a few of the members' comments as well as our thoughts:

James: "I was moved and I didn't expect that. I feel a little naked."
(What does he mean by feeling naked? Does he have regrets? We would encourage him to bring this up either now or at the beginning of the next session.)
SusAnne: "I'd like to work on issues."
(This is a vague and global statement that doesn't tell us much. We ask her to specify the issues and she responds with "trust issues." This is still global, so we ask again and finally she identifies intimate relationships with males.)
Jackie: "I feel a lot safer now. Tomorrow, I would like to work on my feeling inadequate."
(We would ask her to reiterate what she did to bring about this increased safety. And we ask her to briefly identify if there was a time today when she felt inadequate and, if so, at what point.)
Jacqueline: "I was surprised at the work I did today."
(In one sentence, we ask her to identify what was most surprising to her.)

Let us stress that this is not the time for getting into extensive discussion, but for wrapping up a few significant events. Here we are attempting to get members to be more specific and to give one-sentence replies. We can also get a commitment from members at this time if they are willing to bring up a certain issue in the following session. In general, the members perceived the room as a safer place and gave indications of being willing to talk out loud about what they were thinking and feeling. With this willingness to make themselves known, we felt hopeful about the progress of the group.

1. Of the comments made above by SusAnne, Jackie, Jacqueline, and James, which one of them most catches your interest? What would be your reply to this person?

_____

_____

_____

2. What would you say or do if a member of your group were to tell you that he or she feels cut off abruptly by you as you are attempting to close a group session, with just a few minutes remaining?

_____

_____

3. Assume a member says, "I didn't feel that we accomplished anything today. Frankly, I was pretty bored but didn't say anything because I didn't want to offend anyone." What would be your response?

_____

_____

_____

4. What are your thoughts regarding closure for a group session?

_____

_____

_____

5. What specific leadership skills do you think are particularly important to utilize as you are ending a group meeting?

_____

_____

_____

OPENING AND CLOSING A GROUP SESSION

Checking-in Process. As you can see from the video we make interventions to help members focus on how they can best involve themselves in each group session. We don't simply zero in on the first member who speaks, without first giving everyone a chance to participate in a check-in process. Typically, we expect all members to participate in a quick go-around so that we are able to create at least a tentative agenda based on the common concerns of members. Sometimes we structure the check in by asking members to each address a specific question. Below are a few examples of ways to start a group session.

- "What are you aware of most wanting for yourself for this particular session?"
- "Do any of you have thoughts about last week's session or any unfinished business from then that you want to bring up now?"
- "What were you aware of as you were getting ready to come to group?"
- "Have you thought about anything that you explored at the last session?"
- "I'd like to have a go-around in which each of you completes the sentence, 'Right now I am aware of . . .' "

1. What do you consider to be most essential in *opening* a session of a particular group you may lead? How would you modify what you do based upon the population of your group?

_____

_____

_____

2. What specific leadership skills are most essential in the opening of a group session?

_____

_____

_____

Checking-out Process. You'll notice in the video that at the end of a day (a series of sessions for this particular group) we asked members to participate in a check-out process by saying how the day was for each of them. We ask them to identify some of the highlights of the sessions, and also give them a chance to mention any topics they want to put on their agenda for the next session. We do not simply engage in intense work right up until the end of the session. Instead, we intervene in ways to assist members to bring closure on what they experienced. A few examples of questions that we often use as catalysts for assisting members to say a few words about what has been most meaningful to them in a session follow.

- "Are there any ways in which you'd like to be different in the next session than you were in this one?"
- "Even though we have been together for only a short time, what are you learning about yourself?"
- "Are you seeing any of your concerns reflected by others as they are talking?"

Generally, it is good to get members to reflect on what is occurring within the group. We do not want to end abruptly, with little or no closure. Hearing even a few brief comments from every person provides the pulling together that is necessary as the group evolves.

1. What do you consider to be most essential in *closing* a session of a particular group you may lead? How would you modify what you do based upon the population of your group?

_____

_____

_____

2. What do you do with a member who claims to be unfinished with a particular issue at the closing of a session?

_____

_____

_____

REFERENCES

For a more detailed discussion of opening and closing group sessions, see *Groups: Process and Practice* (Chapter 5), and also see *Group Techniques* (Chapter 4, pages 72–75). For ideas of possible lines group leaders can use at the initial stage, see *Student Manual for Theory and Practice of Group Counseling* (Chapter 4).

COREYS' COMMENTARY: THE TRANSITION STAGE

Before groups progress to a working stage, they typically go through what we refer to as a transitional phase, which is characterized by anxiety, defensiveness, resistance, the struggle for control, and inter-member conflicts. During the transitional phase, it is the members' task to monitor their thoughts, feelings, and actions and to learn to express them verbally. Through a manner of being respectful, leaders can help members come to recognize and accept their resistance yet, at the same time, push themselves to challenge their tendencies toward avoidance. For members to progress to a deeper level of exploration, it is necessary that they talk about any anxiety and resistance they may be experiencing. Members make decisions regarding taking risks about bringing out into the open some ways they may be holding back, either out of what they might think of themselves or what others could think of them if they were to reveal themselves more. Some fears of members during an early stage and a transition stage, which are related to resistance, include the fear of: rejection, losing control, being inappropriate, being involved in a conflict, and looking foolish. It is important that group leaders understand there is a purpose for any resistance, and that above all, resistance needs to be respected, understood, and explored.

While leaders should not attack resistance, it is a mistake to bypass or ignore resistive behaviors. Some groups remain stuck at a transitional phase because resistance is unnoticed, ignored, or poorly dealt with by the group leader. Teaching members how to challenge themselves is a basic task at this time, yet it is also essential that members learn how to respectfully confront others in a caring and constructive fashion. We teach members the importance of talking more about themselves and how they are affected by the behaviors of a member they are confronting, rather than telling a member how he or she is or judging that person. We hope we model how to remain open and non-defensive in receiving feedback from others. If conflicts arise, it is essential that members recognize these conflicts and develop the skills to resolve them. Again, what leaders model about addressing conflict in a firm and respectful manner is every bit as important as what they tell members about conflict resolution. If conflict is not addressed, it then becomes a hidden agenda, which blocks open group interaction. How group leaders intervene is crucial to the further building of trust.

During the initial stage, members generally address their fears or reservations about participating in the group. However, during the transition phase, there is a more extensive and more specific discussion of how these fears are manifested within the group. Doing this enables members to feel the support and safety that is required for the intense work they are getting ready to do.

14 Transition Stage

Checking In With Members

We often open a new session, especially during the early phase of a group, with a brief dyad. This serves as a focusing exercise by assisting members to gain clarity on what they want from a particular session. We are attempting to make the members responsible for what they want to bring up for exploration, rather than relying on us to determine their agenda. We also invite them to mention any unfinished business from the previous session. After participants have had a chance to talk in pairs for a few minutes, we reconvene as a group and each member is expected to declare a specific problem area he or she is ready to examine. We also typically add, "Is there anything in your awareness that keeps you from being present in this group at this moment?" We raise this question because sometimes members are distracted by something that has happened in between sessions. Unless they take the opportunity to at least mention what is on their mind, full participation is hindered.

During the check-in time, our aim is to hear what each person most wants to say briefly. We may stay with a member a bit longer to assist him or her in clarifying a goal or solicit more information. At times members become quite emotional as they describe a concern they want to address. In this case, we are apt to say, "Even as you describe your concern, it brings up a lot of pain. I hope that after the check in with everybody that you will claim time to take care of yourself. Is it okay with you if we continue with our go-around right now?" We generally do not stay with any one member before we have completed the check-in process because we want all the members to have a chance to express what they are bringing to this session. Our aim is to identify common themes emerging within the group and to link the work of several members. Below are some comments made by members in the video during the check-in time.

- Jyl mentions her tendency to isolate at times and adds that she would be disappointed if she did not do some work with her father.
- James says that he feels more present and closer to the group.
- Jackie declares that she would like to focus on her feelings of not being good enough.
- SusAnne again brings up her concerns pertaining to trust toward the group.
- Darren is feeling some energy with his dad. (Darren selects Jerry as a symbolic dad for later on).
- Casey is afraid that people will judge her.
- Andrew states that he wants to explore his feelings of betrayal, his feelings of not being good enough, and how he keeps people out of his life. (Andrew picks Jyl as the person that could be helpful for him, because both of them have father issues).

During the check in, Andrew mentions that he and Jyl have been talking between sessions. This kind of sub-grouping between members does not have to be problematic as long as they are willing to bring into the group the essence of what transpired in their discussions. However, sub-grouping is divisive when members discuss perceptions and reactions to others, yet fail to bring this to the entire group.

1. What advantages can you see in utilizing a check-in procedure for beginning a group session?

_____

_____

_____

2. Assume you are facilitating a check in at the beginning of a meeting and as Darren mentions that he wants to explore his relationship with his father, he begins to cry. What do you do or say?

_____

_____

_____

3. At the check in assume that Jyl says, "Last week I left feeling very disappointed because even though I stated I wanted to talk about my father, we never got around to my issue. Frankly, I felt cheated." What would be your response?

_____

_____

_____

4. After several weeks have gone by, at the check in Jackie says she never brings up her issues. She has a hard time believing that she is good enough to ask for group time. What are you likely to say to her?

_____

5. In the groups you expect to lead, how would you help the members get focused and identify their concerns at the beginning of a session?

_____

_____

_____

6. How would you handle the situation if you discovered that several members meet regularly between sessions, yet not everyone is included?

_____

_____

_____

15
Transition Stage

Furthering of Trust Building

After each of the members has checked in, what perks our interest is the lack of trust that SusAnne feels in the group, especially since she has mentioned this before. Because this is a present, here-and-now reaction pertaining to the group, we encourage SusAnne to give expression to her level of trust in us. She informs us that she trusts us somewhat, but does not feel close. We ask her to address each of us individually and say something about the degree to which she trusts each person. Because SusAnne states that people might not be interested in her, we suggest that she make a go-around (including each person in this group) by completing this statement: "You wouldn't be interested in me because . . . " She picked two people whom she felt she could trust, yet did not feel close to. Again, SusAnne was asked to talk to each of them individually and indicate how her feelings toward them might get in the way of her doing work. By acknowledging her doubts and fears, and by discussing them with individuals in the group, she was able to establish the trust necessary for her to get involved in some significant and intensive work later in the group.

Notice that we did not ignore SusAnne's reservations, nor did we encourage group members to offer reassurance to her that they were trustworthy. The core of the struggle lies within SusAnne and she needs to decide if she is willing to take the risk of trusting the members. By making this decision out loud, she includes the people in the group with whom she has doubts. This process allows SusAnne to come to a greater realization of the projections she places on others. Eventually individuals can reply to SusAnne by letting her know whether her assumptions are indeed a reality from their vantage point. For instance, assume SusAnne says, "Marianne, you wouldn't be interested in me because you are too busy with everyone else." I might respond with, "Yes, I am busy, yet I am very interested in you."

Creating Safety

As Casey begins to talk, she is looking down at the ground. She mentions that she worries about being judged by a couple of people. After asking her to select those people, she names SusAnne and Jacqueline. We direct Casey to talk out loud about the ways in which she fears these individuals might judge her. As she looks at both SusAnne and Jacqueline, Casey says aloud all the things she imagines they might be thinking about her. As leaders, we have a hunch that Casey is getting ready to make some deeper personal disclosures. Therefore, Casey first needs to deal with making the room safe, especially with these two people. As we did with SusAnne, we do not bypass nor ignore her reservations, rather we see this as a key focus of her work at this time. Again, we deal with Casey's fears and projections, rather than allowing members to reassure her that she has nothing to fear from them. This demonstrates how we work with members (SusAnne and Casey) to get them ready to do more intensive work at a later session.

Assume you are leading this group, which is in the transition stage, and SusAnne says, "I have a hard time trusting people in this group. I am afraid that people will judge me."

1. How would you be inclined to respond to SusAnne's assumption that you would not be interested in her?

_____

_____

_____

2. What techniques might you employ as a way of helping SusAnne work through her fear and her trust issue?

_____

_____

_____

3. How would you deal with members who could feel rejected or offended by SusAnne's comment that she has a difficult time trusting people in the group?

_____

_____

_____

4. What intervention would you make if several other members joined in with SusAnne and stated that they too had difficulty trusting this group?

_____

_____

_____

5. What would you be inclined to do or say if SusAnne made this remark five minutes before the end of a session?

_____

_____

_____

6. Assume you were a member of this group and you were experiencing a difficult time trusting others. What would you find helpful at this point?

_____

_____

_____

7. In the scenario described on the previous page, Casey has concerns about both SusAnne and Jacqueline and expresses her fear that they might judge her. What intervention would you make?

_____

_____

_____

COREYS' COMMENTARY: MORE ON THE TRANSITION STAGE

During the initial stage of a group the feelings of safety and trust tend to be somewhat generalized. However, during the transition phase, members have had opportunities to observe others, form assumptions about with whom they have reservations, and have developed more intense projections toward others in the room. The anxiety is higher because members are beginning to take more risks by letting themselves be known on a deeper level. For example, it was essential that both SusAnne and Casey dealt with their here-and-now feelings to do the very intense therapeutic work that follows in later sessions. What took place in this session was a process of checking-in, making the room safe, talking about hesitations, and being more specific about what each member's agenda would be. This process of identifying and exploring what could hold members back is essential for a group to evolve into a deeper phase of interpersonal work. If there is a hidden agenda, such as unresolved conflicts, then members are not likely to engage in significant risk taking.

It needs to be mentioned that no arbitrary dividing lines exist between the phases of a group. In actual practice these phases merge with each other. This is especially true of the movement from the transition stage to the working stage. The line between expressing anxieties and ways of avoiding, which is so characteristic of the transition stage, and of working through resistance to move the group into a more advanced stage of development is somewhat thin. If a group does move into the working stage, it can be expected that earlier themes of trust, conflict, and reluctance to participate will surface from time to time. As a group takes on new challenges, deeper levels of trust have to be achieved. Also, considerable conflicts may be settled at the initial stage, yet new conflicts may emerge as the group evolves into the transition and working stages. A group can be compared to an intimate relationship. Neither is static, but both can be characterized as a fluid process. Perfection is never achieved in a group, for smooth waters often turn into stormy waters for a time. Commitment is necessary to do the difficult work of moving forward.

Even if a group eventually reaches a working stage, this does not imply that all members are able to function at the same level of intensity. Some members may be on the periphery, others may still be holding back, and others may be more resistant or less willing to take risks. Indeed, there are individual differences among members at all of the stages of a group. As you will see, some members may be very willing to engage in intensive emotional exploration, which can have the effect of drawing some of the more hesitant members into active participation.

SUMMARY OF THE TRANSITION STAGE

Basic Characteristics of the Transition Stage. The transitional phase of a group's development is marked by feelings of anxiety and defensiveness in the form of various resistances. At this time members:

- wonder about others' acceptance or rejection of them
- test the leader and other members to determine how safe the environment is
- struggle with whether to remain on the periphery or to risk getting involved
- experience some struggle for control and power and some conflict with other members or the leader
- learn how to work through conflict and confrontation
- feel reluctant to get fully involved in working on their personal concerns because they are not sure others in the group will care about them
- observe the leaders to determine if they are trustworthy
- learn how to express themselves so that others will listen to them

Member Functions. A central role of members at this time is to recognize and deal with the many forms of resistance. Tasks include:

- recognizing and expressing the range of feelings
- respecting one's own resistance but working with it
- taking increased responsibility for what they are doing in the group
- learning how to confront others in a constructive manner
- recognizing unresolved feelings from the past as they are being acted out in relation to the group leader or other members
- being willing to face and deal with reactions toward what is occurring in the here-and-now group
- being willing to work through conflicts, rather than avoiding them

Leader Functions. Perhaps the central challenge that leaders face during the transition phase is the need to intervene in the group in a sensitive manner and at the appropriate time. The basic task is to provide both the encouragement and the challenge necessary for the members to face and resolve the conflicts that exist within the group and their own defenses against anxiety and resistance.

Some of the major tasks that leaders need to perform during the transition phase include:

- teaching group members the importance of recognizing and expressing their anxieties
- helping participants recognize the ways in which they react defensively and creating a climate in which they can deal with their resistance openly
- noticing signs of resistance and communicating to the participants that some of these resistances are both natural and healthy
- teaching members the value of recognizing and dealing openly with conflicts that occur in the group

- providing a model for the members by dealing directly and honestly with any challenges to you as a person or as a professional
- encouraging members to express reactions that pertain to here-and-now happenings in the sessions

REFERENCES

For a discussion of the characteristics of a group at the transition stage, difficult group members, interventions for dealing with resistance, and member and leader functions at the transition stage, see *Groups: Process and Practice* (Chapter 6). For a discussion of techniques for dealing with difficult members, dealing with conflict, exploring fears and resistance, and working with challenges to leaders, see *Group Techniques* (Chapter 5). For a summary of issues pertaining to the transition stage of a group's development, see *Theory and Practice of Group Counseling* (Chapter 4, text and student manual). For a discussion of applying different theoretical perspectives in working with themes emerging from the video group, see *Theory and Practice of Group Counseling* (Chapter 17, text and student manual).

QUESTIONS ON APPLYING THE SUMMARY LIST

Now that you have watched this segment of the group during its transitional stage, apply the above summary list to the following questions concerning the video group.

1. What are the *main characteristics* of this group at the transition stage?

_____

_____

_____

2. What *member functions* do you see being illustrated? As you observe the members, what stands out most for you at this phase of the group?

_____

_____

_____

3. Which member (or members) stands out most for you in this segment, and why?

_____

_____

_____

4. What *leader functions* do you see being illustrated? What specific skills and interventions are the co-leaders using at this phase of the group?

_____

_____

_____

5. What are you learning about co-leading a group by observing Marianne and Jerry co-lead this group?

_____

_____

_____

6. What are you learning about how groups either function or malfunction at this point?

_____

_____

_____

Take time to think about a particular kind of group, composed of a specific client population, that you are interested in designing and leading. Answer the following questions from that vantage point.

1. What *specific characteristics* might you expect at the transition stage of the group's development?

_____

_____

_____

2. What *member functions* do you see as being most important at the transition stage?

_____

_____

_____

3. What *leader functions* would you identify as being most crucial at this transition stage?

_____

_____

_____

4. At this phase in your group, what are three group leadership skills you see as being especially important? Which of these skills are strong areas for you? Which skills need improvement?

_____

_____

_____

5. What are the *main challenges* you expect to face at this stage in your group's development?

_____

_____

_____

6. If you were co-leading, what would you most want to talk with your co-leader about at this point in your group's development?

_____

_____

_____

QUESTIONS FOR DISCUSSION AND REFLECTION

1. Members typically display some forms of resistance in a group as a way of coping with anxiety. What are your thoughts on ways to best work with members' resistance? How would you respect resistance? How could you help members explore patterns of resistance?
2. How could you help members understand the purpose of their resistance?
3. During the transition stage, members often express that they are holding back from expressing themselves. What ideas do you have that could lead to more open expression? How might members challenge themselves to say more of what they are thinking and feeling?
4. How ready do you think you are to deal effectively with conflicts in a group situation?
5. What would you have learned about yourself had you been a member or a leader of a group such as this one?
6. What ethical issues can you raise concerning this segment of the group?

PART 4 Working Stage

SELF-INVENTORY TO COMPLETE BEFORE VIEWING THE WORKING STAGE

Directions: The purpose of the self-inventory is to help you identify and clarify your attitudes and beliefs about the variety of group process concepts, techniques, and issues in group leadership. Each of the statements on the inventory is not simply right or wrong, true or false. The point is to get you in an active frame of mind as you watch and reflect on the video and as you complete the workbook activities. Your task is to decide the degree to which you agree or disagree with these statements. Then, after reading the chapter, look over your responses to see whether you want to modify them in any way. This self-inventory will help you express your views and will prepare you to actively read and think about the ideas you'll encounter in this section.

Using the following code, write next to each statement the number of the response that most closely reflects your viewpoint:

5 = I *strongly agree* with this statement.
4 = I *agree*, in most respects, with this statement.
3 = I am *undecided* in my opinion about this statement.
2 = I *disagree*, in most respects, with this statement.
1 = I *strongly disagree* with this statement.

_____ 1. A sign of a working stage involves the free interchange of the members without prodding from the leader.

_____ 2. If my group does not reach a working stage, then I'll feel like I've failed the members and myself.

_____ 3. I associate the working stage with a great deal of emotional expression and catharsis.

_____ 4. Actually, I think there is a fine line between the transition and the working stage.

_____ 5. It is best if one member at a time works with the leader, rather than complicate things by having more than one member at a time work.

_____ 6. One of the more powerful ways to engage members in significant work is to ask them to role-play (or enact) a struggle in the group situation.

_____ 7. Once the group reaches a working stage, there is really no need to monitor trust issues.

_____ 8. During the working stage I would be the most active and directive as a leader.

_____ 9. The aim of the working stage should be to teach members problem-solving strategies.

_____ 10. If a group reaches the working stage, this means that all the members are at the same level of self-exploration.

17

Working Stage

Who Wants to Work?

After Jerry asks who wants to make use of the group time, James jumps in immediately. Although he says he wants time, he is ambivalent and attempts to shift the focus onto SusAnne, asking her to work in the hopes that she would trigger his work. We intervene with this attempt. If James wants to work, he should not put another member on the spot. He then asks SusAnne if she is willing to role-play a former girlfriend, and she agrees. Even though James gets a green light from SusAnne and us, he hesitates indicating that he jumped in too soon and that we should go to someone else. At this juncture, we are not invested in keeping the spotlight on James, who lets us know that he does not feel ready to proceed.

1. What did you think about the leader's intervention by shifting the focus to someone else when James said he wasn't ready to work?

   _____

   _____

   _____

2. A member (SusAnne) tells you she wants to work, yet she keeps herself very vague and global regarding what she wants to explore. What do you say to her?

   _____

   _____

   _____

3. You are leading a group and ask, "Who wants to work?" There is a long silence and nobody gives any indication of wanting to talk about any area of personal concern. What assumptions could you draw from this situation?

   _____

   _____

   _____

18

Working Stage

Commentary on Casey's Work

At this point, Casey indicates her eagerness to continue what she began in an earlier session and we shift our focus to her. Casey is most aware of SusAnne and what she might think of her as she gets ready to make a significant disclosure. Casey acknowledges her projections about being judged negatively by SusAnne. Then Casey proceeds to tell SusAnne that she is gay.

Again, we can see how essential it is that Casey establishes a firm basis of trust in the room. She is taking a tremendous risk in disclosing that she is gay. At this point, she does not know how the people in the group will react to her, especially SusAnne and Jacqueline, whom she singled out earlier. Even though we may not say much to Casey as she is sharing, she needs to feel our presence and support. Later in her work, she acknowledged that she was aware of Marianne's presence, and that she felt supported. Although Casey feared judgments from the group members, she finds people to be very caring and accepting. We direct her to look around the room to ensure that this support registers with her and we challenge her to remember what she sees in members' faces. Later on, should Casey slip into judging herself, hopefully she can call to mind the supportive feedback she received from everyone.

19
Working Stage

Symbolic Exploration Through Role-Playing

Casey's work takes a different turn when she expresses her sadness about having to keep her being gay a secret from her mother. Casey proceeds, yet is obviously frightened. Jerry suggests a role play involving Casey picking a person in the group to be her symbolic mother. We observe considerable hesitation on Casey's part. Marianne doesn't want Casey to feel pressured to move ahead with the role play and asks, "Is this your agenda or Jerry's?" She lets it be known that she is scared, yet she wants to continue. Casey agrees with Marianne that it would be more meaningful to role-play with her mother in her native language (Vietnamese). We continue to find that when people role-play with significant others in their primary language other than English, the outcome of the therapeutic engagement is often more productive. It is not necessary that those in the room understand the content of what is being conveyed. What is important is that this therapeutic dialogue has meaning to the client. Those who observe the work are typically affected emotionally even though they do not understand what is being said.

Casey, who picks Marianne as her symbolic mother, first reveals that she is gay. We follow Casey's lead who eventually says, "I keep thinking what my mother would say back to me." Marianne asks Casey to reverse roles, "becoming her mother," and express what she imagines her mother would tell her about this disclosure. After this exchange, Casey makes a comment about what a "good mother" would say. Again, taking the cue from Casey, Marianne suggests that Casey become the "good mother" and tell Marianne (who assumes the role of Casey) what she knows that Casey needs to hear.

It needs to be mentioned that in reality, Casey may never tell her mother about her sexual orientation, nor would we as co-leaders ever push her to do so. What she tells her mother, if anything, must be her choice. Certainly, we would not tell Casey to go out and say everything she expressed symbolically in the therapeutic situation. Instead, if she decides to actually open a dialogue with her mother, she needs to decide what she most wants to say to her, and what the price might be if she does. Even if Casey does not actually approach her mother, her therapeutic enactment was both cathartic and healing. Ideally, Casey would like to have the "good mother" she deserves, yet at this time, she made a fine start by symbolically saying to herself what she would so much like to hear from her mother. Casey's mother may never be able to agree with Casey's decisions of how she wants to live her life, yet Casey can come to an affirmation of herself as a person. A very important outcome of Casey's work was the realization that her catastrophic expectations (negatives judgments from the members) were not reality based. Marianne plants a seed in Casey's mind that maybe her mother, like the group, may not be as condemning of her as she fears. The stakes for Casey are high, and what to do with her mother will present some difficulties for her. Another result of her work was her decision to be a bit more trusting with select people about who she is.

It is to be noted that although the video contains a relatively large segment of Casey's therapy, the actual session lasted over an hour. As can be seen, Casey's emotional work proves to be a catalyst for most of the other members. We, as leaders, were also emotionally touched, and generally we do not hesitate to disclose this. Just because we become emotional does not imply that we lose our objectivity and are unable to facilitate the members' interactions.

REFERENCE

For a more detailed illustration of using a member's native language in a symbolic role play, see *Group Techniques* (Chapter 6, pages 131–132).

1. What reactions did you have as you observed the session in which Casey did an intensive piece of work? What aspects of her work most affected you, and why? How would this have helped or hindered you in working with her?

_____

_____

_____

2. What reactions did you have toward Casey when she disclosed she was gay? What might you have said to her after this disclosure?

_____

_____

_____

3. Assume that after Casey disclosed that she was gay one of the members said the following: "Casey, I need to let you know that I have a hard time hearing this, because I'm not comfortable with homosexuality." How would you intervene?

_____

_____

_____

4. In a role play, Casey spoke to her symbolic mother in Vietnamese? As she did so, what, if anything, did you notice about her body language?

_____

_____

_____

5. Considering Casey's cultural background, would you have any concerns for her if she indicated her intention to tell her mother that she is gay? What would you say to her?

_____

_____

_____

6. What would you say if several group members began pressuring Casey to talk to her mother in real life and let her know about her sexual orientation?

_____

_____

_____

7. Marianne was emotionally affected by Casey's work, and let her know about this. What would you do or say if you became emotionally involved in a member's work?

_____

_____

_____

8. From observing Marianne and Jerry co-leading during this segment, what did you learn that you could apply?

_____

_____

_____

Involving Other Members In Intensive Work

Although not shown in the video, in later sessions every member did some emotionally-laden work and engaged in significant and insightful self-exploration. Much of that work was triggered by the earlier work of others. Only brief segments of some of the members' work can be seen in the video. On the following pages we highlight ways that other members brought themselves into the session by addressing their struggles.

REFERENCE

For a description of working with several members who simultaneously experience intense emotions, see *Group Techniques* (Chapter 6, pages 126–128).

20
Working Stage

Jyl's Loss of Her Father

Some of Jyl's unfinished business with her father pertains to the fact that when she was growing up he communicated to her that she could never become the great pianist that she thought she could become. Instead, he waited until the day before he died to tell her that she could have made it. This leads Jyl to explore the possibility that it is not too late for her to resume her career as a pianist. One of Jyl's issues is that she tends to withdraw in social interactions. She gets the insight that she could use playing the piano as a way to reach out and make contact with others. Jyl makes a contract to do this before the follow-up session for this group.

1. Given what you saw of Jyl in the video, how might you pursue work with her if she wanted to talk about her sadness over her father not telling her earlier that she could have made it as a pianist?

_____

_____

_____

2. How would you decide what to focus on with Jyl? Would you focus on her sadness over losing her father? Her issues with men? Her disappointment of not having become a pianist? What would guide you in your decision?

_____

_____

_____

21
Working Stage

Never Good Enough

Jackie is very affected as she talks about working so hard on being perfect and pleasing everybody, never making anyone mad, and never feeling like she is enough. During a go-around she explores how hard she tries to be entertaining, witty, funny, pretty, and never boring. As a result of her exploration in group, she realizes that she has always felt responsible for her mother's leaving, even at the age of seven. Although Jackie realizes on a cognitive level that she wasn't responsible for her mother leaving, on an emotional level, she is still not convinced. Jackie's insights into her dynamics can help her to more readily recognize those instances when she exhausts herself by attempting to be everything to everybody.

1. Jackie talks about trying to please others and to be perfect. To what degree can you identify with her issue? How might this help or hinder you in facilitating her work?

_____

_____

_____

2. Given that Jackie has insight into her behavior, what kinds of homework might you suggest in collaboration with her?

_____

_____

_____

22
Working Stage

Wanting Approval

Jacqueline initially brought up her need for universal approval. In this session, she gets in touch with her pain over trying to connect with her mother, and getting her mother's approval. She role-plays with Marianne as her symbolic mother, which leads to insight regarding how she often expects people around her to approve of her in the way her mother never did.

1. Jacqueline talks about striving to get her mother's approval. To what degree have you been concerned about parental approval? How might this help or hinder you in facilitating her work?

_____

_____

_____

2. Given that Jacqueline is an African-American woman, how might you take this into consideration as you work with her issue of seeking approval?

_____

_____

_____

REFERENCE

For a discussion of utilizing techniques in dealing with the theme, "I so much want your approval", see *Group Techniques* (Chapter 6, pages 138–139).

Linking Members by Role-playing

In the actual group, but not shown in the video, James and Jackie engage in a very long role play in which Jackie symbolically talks to James as her son and James talks to Jackie as his mother. Both are helped by this role play. James has an opportunity to express some words he rarely says to his mother. Eventually, he contracts to spend some time with his mother and to tell her how much he appreciates her and cares for her. Jackie receives the longed-for recognition and appreciation that she so much desires from her son. She provides feedback to James, hoping that he will indeed talk to his mother, and lets James know how good it felt to hear his words. This interchange between Jackie and James illustrates how transference in groups, if tapped, can be productive in helping members explore places they are stuck in significant relationships. We pay close attention to transference and look for ways to link members who can be therapeutically useful to each other. Those symbolic enactments in the group frequently lead to a new direction in their interpersonal relationships outside of the group.

1. Who else in the group could be invited into the dialogue between Jackie and James?

_____

_____

_____

2. What might you say to draw in other members into the above dialogue?

_____

_____

_____

23 Working Stage

Working With Metaphors

We also pay close attention to words, phrases, and metaphors that members use to describe themselves. Darren is affected by the symbolic enactments with parental figures. He already has some insight into the parallels between his relationship with his parents and how he often feels with people in this group. He feels that his mother has a hard time in seeing him as an adult, and likewise, he sees himself in the group as a kid that tries to fit in. Darren says, "I wish I had more of a relationship with my parents. It gets in my way with people in this group. It feels like a 'hole in my soul.'" After he continues talking for awhile, Marianne draws his attention to what appeared to be a significant phrase. Marianne says, "You said an important word. I experience it as a 'hole in my soul.' Do you want to look at a few people and repeat that sentence?"

Darren looks at different members and says, "It feels like a hole in my soul. I blame myself for it, like there is something wrong with me." As can be seen in the video, Darren gets intensely emotional as he taps into some painful childhood memories. He is crying and looking down at the floor. Marianne suggests that he pick a person that would be helpful for him to make contact with as he continues talking. He picks Jyl and begins talking to her as Jyl, and then shifts and addresses her as his mother. Darren talks to Jyl, "I wish you could have been there for me." Marianne says, "Keep looking at her, even though it is hard."

Darren continues, "I had to do everything by myself. I was scared and lonely. I wanted to tell someone how I felt. I feel so alone with my feelings. And I still feel that way a lot. I don't know how to show my feelings." Marianne interjects, "You are showing a lot of feelings now." Darren looks at her and says, "Yes." He continues, "It was hard growing up that way." Marianne's comment is aimed at reinforcing Darren's expression of deep feelings, since Darren just said that he is unable to do so. We often note and give members feedback when they are demonstrating a behavior that they claim they cannot do.

Typically, we ask members to look at and talk to a particular person in the group, whether or not that individual reminds them of a significant other. We want members to be aware of the supportive presence that is often in the room. This supportive connection generally enables them to take the risks involved in going to scary places, as was the case with Darren.

Jerry made an intervention as Darren was speaking, "How old do you feel now?" Darren picked about seven years old. Jerry asks Darren to continue talking, but as the seven-year-old child. This gives us important information about Darren's experiences as a child and possible decisions he made at that time which are now interfering with his adult life. He is currently operating on old decisions, some of which are no longer functional. As a child he felt lonely, and now in this group he doubts that he fits in. This causes him to be hesitant with people in this group as well as in his outside life. Consequently, what he tells himself keeps him lonely. Because of this exploration, Darren becomes keenly aware of the ways in which he expects people to treat him the way his family responded to him. With the awareness of how he sets up a self-fulfilling prophesy, he can begin to act differently. Instead of shying away from people, he can approach people with the attitude that he has something to offer them and that they might be interested in him.

As you notice in the video, Darren, as well as others, are encouraged to continue talking even though they are crying. We find that it is therapeutic for members to put words to their emotions. There is a great deal of wisdom and truth expressed during moments such as these. We carefully listen to what Darren is saying while he is emotional in order to be able to reflect back and to remind him, at a later point, what he has said. We don't give him words or tell him what to feel. Instead, we pick up sentences and phrases that Darren has said and have him repeat those during a role-play situation, such as the phrase "hole in my soul." Darren reported that his father wasn't there for him. During a role play with his symbolic father, we might tell him to let his father know what it felt like to not have his father there.

Darren expresses a good deal of hurt toward his parents. At some point he suddenly interrupts himself, turns to Marianne and says, "My mom and dad did the best they could with what they had, but it still hurt growing up." We want to be respectful of Darren's needs to protect his parents at that moment. Furthermore, we are likely to discourage group members from talking him out of being understanding of his parents. Darren can be hurt, angry, understanding, and eventually, forgiving. It is important that he gives sufficient expression to his whole range of feelings. These symbolic role plays with parents go beyond blaming one's past for current problems. We see it as being therapeutically valuable to give expression to painful feelings associated with past and present events. Participants typically report a sense of release and healing after expressing bottled-up emotions. The emotional release, coupled with the insight that frequently follows, enables members to make new and more functional decisions about how they want to live.

After members experience a cathartic breakthrough, it is not uncommon for them to report their aware-ness of feeling exposed, embarrassed, naked, and vulnerable. At times like this members sometimes discount the actual work they did and the courage they displayed. What is crucial at these times is to avoid giving quick reassurance, or attempting to talk members out of their feelings. For instance, Jerry asks Darren, "How was it for you to do this work?" Darren lets us know, "It was really hard. I feel that I showed my worst. I feel that I was weak." Now Jerry urges Darren to look at members in the room and to verbalize his concerns, especially what he fears that people might be thinking about him. Looking at people in the room, rather than turning away in embarrassment, enables Darren to note the understanding and compassion that others are feeling toward him. If he gets stuck with his embarrassment, he is likely to discount his insights and begin to criticize himself for "breaking down" in front of others. When Darren is being self-critical, Jerry asks him to reflect on what he thought about others who showed their emotions. Jerry slowly facilitates Darren toward giving himself the kind of understanding and nonjudgmental acceptance that he is willing to give to others.

1. How were you personally affected as you observed Darren's work described above?

_____

_____

_____

2. What are some possibilities you can see in working with Darren's phrase "a hole in my soul?"

_____

_____

_____

3. Assume you are leading the group and after Darren's work he announces, "I'm really feeling vulnerable and so embarrassed. I can't believe that I lost control like that." How might your interventions differ from those of Jerry and Marianne?

_____

_____

_____

4. What therapeutic value, if any, do you see in Darren crying?

_____

_____

_____

5. How do you feel about men showing emotions, and how would this influence your intervention with Darren?

_____

_____

_____

6. Assume another member gives Darren this feedback: "I think you should let go of your past and being so hung up on what your parents didn't give you. It seems to me like you're crying over spilt milk and I can't see what good this is doing." What would you say to this member?

_____

_____

7. What purpose do you see in linking Darren with other members, especially asking him to look at them and talk to them as a seven-year-old?

REFERENCE

For a discussion of utilizing techniques in dealing with the language of members and exploring metaphors, see *Group Techniques* (Chapter 8, pages 174–175).

24
Working Stage

Working With Relationships

Earlier SusAnne spent a considerable amount of time in establishing trust with members. She was able to go beyond her resistance, which was expressed by her lack of clarity and focus. Because she took care of these foundational concerns, she is now able to initiate and negotiate a role play with James as her former boyfriend. SusAnne declares that she keeps a lot of words and feelings inside, which causes her a great deal of physical stress. She agrees that it would be helpful to hear herself say out loud some of the things that she often pounds herself with silently. SusAnne not only verbalizes her pain in this role play with James as her boyfriend, but also is asked to symbolically hand over elements of her pain to him. She very deliberately hands over to him hurt, lies, shame, and guilt. Notice that after SusAnne has given away feelings she's held in, she declares that she feels much lighter, especially in her shoulders.

At this point it is important that a leader checks-in with James concerning how he is affected by what just transpired. It is obvious that he has physical reactions. While SusAnne's shoulders feel lighter, James makes what appears to be out-of-awareness movements with his shoulders, sending a nonverbal message that his shoulders feel burdened. James does not merely role-play with SusAnne as her boyfriend. He taps into his own feelings over a previous relationship with a woman in his life. The role play between SusAnne and James is another example of maximizing transference reactions and getting two people engaged in therapeutic work. As a result of the reciprocal exchange, both SusAnne and James have a sense of relief. SusAnne notes how much better it feels to her when she even temporarily lets go of these painful feelings. She makes a decision that she does not have to keep her feelings bottled up. She is also more open to letting other people into her life without too quickly assuming that they are not to be trusted and that they will hurt her. Furthermore, SusAnne can continue to remind herself how freeing it is when she refuses to accept all the responsibility for what went wrong in her prior relationship. James becomes aware of how important it is to him to have been forgiven in this symbolic role play. Although he realizes that his girlfriend may not be as forgiving, he wants to be able to forgive himself.

At the end of the dialogue between SusAnne and James, he initiates a hug. When James asks the co-leaders for permission, we tell him that he needs to check this out with SusAnne. He does and SusAnne is able to respond. However, had James asked SusAnne for a hug prematurely, when she was expressing her anger and hurt toward him, we would have intervened with his attempts to dissipate the intensity of her feelings. Physical contact among members is often therapeutic, yet it needs to be done in a timely way, and not be done to short-circuit a member's expression and exploration of intense feelings.

We pay attention to the nonverbal communication of members, believing that the way members express themselves is often more important than the content they express. We look for patterns of nonverbal communication, yet we generally avoid quickly interpreting the meaning underlying these messages. Instead, we ask clients to become aware of their own body language and other nonverbal forms of communication and attach their own meanings to what they are expressing bodily. This is particularly illustrated in the exchange between SusAnne and James. You might play the section back after SusAnne hands over to James her feelings, noting what James might be expressing nonverbally.

1. How were you personally affected as you observed SusAnne's work described above?

_____

_____

_____

2. If, as you were leading this group, some of your own unfinished business and pain over a relationship were tapped, how would this affect your ability to facilitate dialogue between SusAnne and James?

_____

_____

_____

3. Assume that several members displayed anger toward James for having hurt a woman in his life. What would you do?

_____

_____

_____

4. Assume that several members insist that SusAnne should show more anger in the role play. What would you do?

_____

_____

_____

5. In the video, SusAnne symbolically gives back to her boyfriend the hurt, shame, and lies she has been carrying around. What therapeutic purpose do you see in this technique?

_____

_____

_____

6. In the video, you can see the nonverbal behavior of James when SusAnne is finished handing over to him the hurt she's been keeping inside. How might you work with the nonverbal behaviors James expresses if you notice this?

_____

_____

_____

7. What do you imagine the outcome of SusAnne's exploration would have been if she simply *talked about* her situation with her ex-boyfriend?

_____

_____

_____

8. From observing Marianne's and Jerry's co-leading during this segment, what did you learn that you could apply?

_____

_____

_____

25
Working Stage

Andrew's Struggle of Keeping Pain Inside

SusAnne and James have achieved closure. Both Marianne and Jerry know that Andrew has also talked about his painful divorce. It is likely that he has been very affected by what transpired between SusAnne and James, yet he does not express what he is feeling. Operating on a hunch, Jerry asks Andrew how he was affected. Indeed, Andrew acknowledges that this interchange brought up his pain over his previous relationship. Jerry asks Andrew to look at and tell SusAnne about how he has been hurt and how he shuts people out. He declines at first, stating that he does not want to get back to that pain. As he puts it, "I want to let my hurt go out the back door. I want to put it in the freezer." However, he does continue to talk about his pain, while staying quite cognitive. He describes his pain graphically with words such as: "It's like I've been stabbed." Jerry asks, "Where?" Andrew replies, "In my core. In my soul and heart. My very sensitive part." It is clear that Andrew labors and is ambivalent over making himself vulnerable with people versus shutting them out and keeping them isolated. Only a small segment of the interchanges with Andrew is seen in the video. His exploration is slow and tedious.

At one point Marianne asks him, "Do you see any hope for yourself?" He replies, "I see a lot of hope. It's just if I will take that key and open the door. I want to open the door a little bit." Marianne asks Andrew how he can let us in a little bit right now in this room. He does not respond to her invitation. Marianne also asks him, "What can you do to avoid being disappointed by the end of the group?" He thinks about this for awhile. Then Marianne teases him, "You sure think a lot. You wear me out! Do you realize how hard I am working with you?" Both Marianne and Andrew laugh. This kind of humor must be timely and should be based on a trusting relationship. Humor must never be at the client's expense, nor should it be aimed at putting them down or embarrassing them. We tend to use humor as a therapeutic leverage, which often helps members put into perspective the meaning they ascribe to a situation.

There is another noteworthy aspect of Andrew's struggle. Andrew comments several times that he isolates and is not able to reach out to people. Yet, he was given feedback by both the leaders and some members that inclined him to be supportive toward a particular member at different junctures during the group, but he stopped himself. For example, when Casey cried, Andrew sat next to her and wanted to reach out to her, yet he stopped himself, which was a pattern for him. It is important that he hears the feedback that it is not true that he is unable to feel for others, but that he holds himself back from doing what he is inclined to do. Therefore, the focus is not to get Andrew to feel, but to get him to express more readily those feelings that do emerge within him. Making himself vulnerable in this way is still a scary step for him to take. At least at this time in his life, he is not sure how much he wants to open himself to others.

At a later session, Andrew and Jerry engage in a role-playing situation whereby Andrew gives voice to his emotional and soft side, while Jerry plays the defiant and critical side. Then when Andrew seems ready to shift, he plays the hard and critical side of himself, while Jerry assumes the gentle and caring side of Andrew. This technique is an illustration of externalizing an internal debate that often goes on within Andrew. At times, we direct members to express out loud what appear to be conflicting sides of themselves. We ask them to stay with one side for some time, and exaggerate that side. Doing so, they are often in a position to decide how they might want to integrate these sides more harmoniously into their personality. Andrew learns that he does not need to live exclusively by one side of himself. As he put it, "There are two parts of me. I would like to mate my gentle and caring side with the fearless and defiant side."

The therapeutic intervention with Andrew's struggle illustrates dealing with polarities. Many of the techniques we use involve the exploration of polarities in members, even though members may not want to acknowledge what seem like opposite sides within them (such as a tender side and a tough side). Many of our techniques ask members to exaggerate one side of themselves a bit longer to get more information about that side and to decide whether it is a way they want to be. Our techniques (like the one with Andrew) are not aimed at getting rid of one of these aspects of self, but to help a member acknowledge a part that may be neglected or rejected.

REFERENCE

For a discussion of utilizing techniques in dealing with the theme, "A part of me wants this, and a part of me wants that", see *Group Techniques* (Chapter 6, pages 137–138).

1. What reactions are evoked in you as you observe and listen to Andrew's pain over his divorce?

_____

_____

_____

2. Andrew says, "It's like I've been stabbed, in my heart and my core." What possibilities do you see of working with his symbolic and powerful words?

_____

_____

3. What would you tend to focus on in your work with Andrew, and why? What outcome would you hope for?

_____

_____

_____

4. Andrew says, "I want to let my hurt go out the back door. I want to put it in the freezer." How might you intervene?

_____

_____

_____

5. Assume that another member were to say to Andrew, "Get out of your head and get into your gut! I'm tired of your head trips!" How would you intervene?

_____

_____

_____

COREYS' COMMENTARY: THE WORKING STAGE

As usual, at the end of this day we ask members to participate in a check out. They make a few remarks about what this day was like for them, how they felt about what they did, and what they are learning from their exploration.

During the sessions you just saw, one member (Casey) comes forth and declares she is ready to do some of the work she came here to do. Much of what followed demonstrates the impact Casey had on other members and how they tapped into their unfinished business with their parents. Even though some of these members did not declare parental issues as a part of their initial agenda, they were drawn into feelings about their parents at this juncture. We often see this occurring in groups and we sometimes mention to members to be prepared to deal with issues that spontaneously emerge.

As is obvious in the video, many members became intensively emotional as they talked about painful experiences as children. This is not uncommon, especially during the working stage of a cohesive group. The emotionality of one member often sparks the emotions of others. However, a group can be productive and meaningful to members, even if a great deal of emotional expression is not present. In some groups there is likely to be an absence of the expression of intense emotions, yet the group can still be functioning well and achieving its goals. The interactions may focus on more subtle and seemingly less dramatic issues, but the key point is that the group is characterized by a willingness to work through material rather than a tendency to shelve issues. We do not want to set up the expectation or establish a norm that for a group to be productive, everybody has to cry or experience a catharsis.

SUMMARY OF THE WORKING STAGE

Basic Characteristics of the Working Stage. When a group reaches the working stage, the central characteristics include the following:

- The level of trust and cohesion is high.
- Communication within the group is open and involves an accurate expression of what is being experienced.
- Members interact with one another freely and directly.
- There is a willingness to risk threatening material and to make oneself known to others; members bring to the group personal topics they want to discuss and understand better.
- Conflict among members is recognized and dealt with directly and effectively.
- Feedback is given freely and accepted and considered nondefensively.
- Confrontation occurs in a way in which those doing the challenging avoid slapping judgmental labels on others.
- Members are willing to work outside the group to achieve behavioral changes.
- Participants feel supported in their attempts to change and are willing to risk new behavior.
- Members feel hopeful that they can change if they are willing to take action; they do not feel helpless.

Member Functions. The working stage is characterized by the exploration of personally meaningful material. To reach this stage, members have certain tasks:

- initiating topics they want to explore
- giving others feedback and being open to receiving it
- sharing how they are affected by others' presence and work in the group
- practicing new skills and behaviors in daily life and bringing the results to the sessions
- offering both challenge and support to others and engaging in self-confrontation
- continually assessing their satisfaction with the group and actively taking steps to change their level of involvement in the sessions if necessary

Leader Functions. Some of the central leadership functions at this stage include:

- providing systematic reinforcement of desired group behaviors that foster cohesion and productive work
- looking for common themes among members' work that provide for some universality
- continuing to model appropriate behavior, especially caring confrontation, and disclosing ongoing reactions to the group
- supporting the members' willingness to take risks and assisting them in carrying this behavior into their daily living
- interpreting the meaning of behavior patterns at appropriate times so that members will be able to reach a deeper level of self-exploration and consider alternative behaviors
- focusing on the importance of translating insight into action
- encouraging members to keep in mind what they want from the group and to ask for it

REFERENCES

For a discussion of moving from the transition to the working stage, characteristics of the working stage, therapeutic factors operating in a group, and member and leader functions at the working stage, see *Groups: Process and Practice* (Chapter 7). For a description of techniques for exploring material and emerging themes for the working stage, see *Group Techniques* (Chapter 6). For a summary of issues pertaining to the working stage of a group's development, see *Theory and Practice of Group Counseling* (Chapter 5, text and student manual). For a discussion of applying different theoretical perspectives in working with themes emerging from the video group, see *Theory and Practice of Group Counseling* (Chapter 17, text and student manual).

QUESTIONS ON APPLYING THE SUMMARY LIST

Now that you have watched this segment of the group during its working stage, apply the above summary list to the following questions concerning the video group.

1. What are the *main characteristics* of this group at the working stage?

_____

_____

_____

2. What *member functions* do you see being illustrated? As you observe the members, what stands out most for you at this phase of the group?

_____

_____

_____

3. Which member (or members) stands out most for you in this segment, and why?

_____

_____

_____

4. What *leader functions* do you see being illustrated? What specific skills and interventions are the co-leaders using at this phase of the group?

_____

_____

_____

5. What are you learning about co-leading a group by observing Marianne and Jerry co-lead this group?

_____

_____

_____

6. What are you learning about how groups either function or malfunction at this point?

_____

_____

_____

Take time to think about a particular kind of group, composed of a specific client population, that you are interested in designing and leading. Answer the following questions from that vantage point.

1. What *specific characteristics* might you expect at the working stage of the group's development?

_____

_____

_____

2. What *member functions* do you see as being most important at the working stage?

_____

_____

_____

3. What *leader functions* would you identify as being most crucial at this working stage?

_____

_____

_____

4. At this phase in your group, what are three group leadership skills you see as being especially important? Which of these skills are strong areas for you? Which skills need improvement?

_____

_____

_____

5. What are the *main challenges* you expect to face at this stage in your group's development?

_____

_____

_____

6. If you were co-leading, what would you most want to talk with your co-leader about at this point in your group's development?

_____

_____

_____

QUESTIONS FOR DISCUSSION AND REFLECTION

1. From what you observed from the video during this phase of group, how ready are you to deal with intense feelings that members might bring out in a group?

2. What value do you see in the expression of emotions in a group?

3. To what degree have you identified in your own life some of the personal issues that the members brought out in the video? To what extent have you explored some of these issues?

4. What do you look for in a group to assess the degree to which that group is engaged in productive work?

5. Up to this point, what are some of the main lessons that you are learning about how to best facilitate interaction among the participants in a group?

6. What would you have learned about yourself had you been a member or a leader of a group such as this one?

7. What ethical issues can you raise concerning this segment of the group?

PART 5 The Ending Stage

SELF-INVENTORY TO COMPLETE BEFORE VIEWING THE ENDING STAGE

Directions: The purpose of the self-inventory is to help you identify and clarify your attitudes and beliefs about the variety of group process concepts, techniques, and issues in group leadership. Each of the statements on the inventory is not simply right or wrong, true or false. The point is to get you in an active frame of mind as you watch and reflect on the video and as you complete the workbook activities. Your task is to decide the degree to which you agree or disagree with these statements. Then, after reading the chapter, look over your responses to see whether you want to modify them in any way. This self-inventory will help you express your views and will prepare you to actively read and think about the ideas you'll encounter in this section.

Using the following code, write next to each statement the number of the response that most closely reflects your viewpoint:

5 = I *strongly agree* with this statement.
4 = I *agree*, in most respects, with this statement.
3 = I am *undecided* in my opinion about this statement.
2 = I *disagree*, in most respects, with this statement.
1 = I *strongly disagree* with this statement.

_____ 1. As a leader, it is my job to assist members in dealing with termination.

_____ 2. I am very much in favor of asking members to evaluate the impact of the group experience at the last meeting.

_____ 3. I am inclined to use structured exercises to assist members in consolidating their learnings.

_____ 4. I would structure some final sessions so that each member both gives and receives feedback.

_____ 5. Scheduling a follow-up meeting seems like a way to soften the difficulties involved in making a separation.

_____ 6. If the group members worked successfully, then conflict would certainly be absent at the ending sessions.

_____ 7. I would have a difficult time saying good-bye if I had become close to the members in a group I was leading.

_____ 8. It is a good idea to ask members to formulate a contract that spells out how they are likely to carry out their learnings in daily life once the group ends.

_____ 9. I would bring up the topic of potentially reverting to old patterns and the tendency to discount what one has learned before the final meeting.

_____ 10. Members will learn more from a group experience if I help them practice interpersonal skills toward the ending phase of group.

26
Ending Stage

Reflecting on Afterthoughts

We open the last day of the group by reminding the members that this is a day for reflecting on what they have accomplished and for spending time talking about how they might carry out their new learnings into their everyday lives. We mention the importance of writing in their journal as a way of keeping track of what they learned, what steps they took in this group to bring about change, and what they want to apply to everyday life. Jerry asks the members if they have any afterthoughts about the work they did the previous day, because if they do, this needs to be brought out and dealt with at least briefly.

From experience, we know that members sometimes have residual feelings about intense emotional work at a subsequent session, and as well, they frequently have new insights associated with their work. Marianne asks the members if they have any regrets about what they did or did not do in an earlier session, or any reactions to other members. It is important to structure sessions during the ending phase that will allow time for exploration of any residual feelings.

1. What uses do you see in journal writing once a group terminates? What would you say to members about the value of keeping a journal as a way to continue self-reflection?

    _____

    _____

    _____

2. What questions would you want to raise in your groups pertaining to possible afterthoughts the members may have had about their experience in group?

    _____

    _____

    _____

27
Ending Stage

Preparing Members for Termination

At this ending stage, our task as co-leaders is to prepare members for termination. It is important to remind members about the limited time left so that they can bring closure to the group experience. We give members adequate time to share and work through their feelings and thoughts about termination of the group. It is essential that they identify any unfinished business pertaining to the group in advance of the final group session. We tell members that the last meeting is neither the time to introduce new work, nor is it the time to bring up reactions to others that they have kept to themselves for the course of the entire group. Some of the questions we ask members as the group moves toward termination are:

- What were a few of the turning points in this group for you?
- What most stands out for you about being in this group?
- What is it like for you to realize that shortly this group will end?
- What would you like to take away from this group and use in your life?
- What contracts do you want to make?
- How you can use others in the group as a source of support?

1. How well do you think you are able to deal with termination issues in a group? What personal difficulties, if any, might you have in accepting the ending of a group?

_____

_____

_____

2. What are some of your ideas regarding how you can prepare members for dealing with endings?

_____

_____

_____

3. If you could raise only three questions for the members of your group to discuss at the final session, what would these questions be?

_____

_____

_____

Consolidation of Learnings

Some specific statements about the group by members, along with a brief comment on our part, are given below:

Darren: "I feel so much better now."

(Remembering that Darren stated earlier his concerns about being perceived as weak if he were to cry, Jerry asks him if he has any thoughts or feelings about the time in group that he cried and expressed some painful childhood memories. Darren is not critical of expressing his emotions and adds that what helped him was to check out the group after he completed an intense piece of work earlier. We also challenge Darren and others who may have a tendency to be critical of what they said or did in a group to consider what they might do when they no longer have the support of the group. Although Darren talks about his reactions to expressing himself emotionally and eventually feels better about doing this, later he may begin to experience doubts and wonder if what he did was "weak." If Darren is self-critical of showing emotion, it would be useful for him to practice talking back to the critical inner voices during a group session, and then continue to practice challenging his negative self-talk outside the group.)

Jackie: "I realize that I am not so boring and I'm not as critical of myself. Now I see that some areas where I was the most critical are really my assets. Now I'm able to feeling nurturing from you."
(We want to know what it is like for her to allow herself to receive nurturance from others, since this is a shift for her. We also ask her what she did that resulted in her being more accepting of herself.)
Andrew: "The cognitive role play that I did helped me see that there are both soft and hard sides of me."
(We challenge Andrew to continue reflecting on which side of himself he wants to express more frequently. We ask him to consider the emotional price of keeping people out and remaining emotionally tough.)

SusAnne explored some issues pertaining to her mother, as well as her former boyfriend, yet the work she did with her mother was not in the video. She has more clarity on what she would want to say to her mom, and she would like to be able to initiate a different kind of dialogue with her.

At this juncture, we could give SusAnne an opportunity to engage in a brief behavioral rehearsal where she picks a mom from the group and makes a few key statements that she wants her mom to really hear. We need to let members know that this is not the time for extensive exploration, but more for identifying a few specific things she might say in a future discussion with her mother.

Consider the statements made by the group members above and assume that you are the leader of this group. Also, assume that these comments were made by way of a summary check in at one of the sessions during the ending phase of your group. Once the check in is completed, consider how you might intervene with each member if they were ready to do further work, given the group is moving toward termination.

1. SusAnne says, "I have a clearer idea of what I want to say to my mom." What direction would you go with SusAnne?

    _____

    _____

    _____

2. Jackie says, "I am now more able to receive nurturing from you all." What ways might you connect this with her life outside of group?

    _____

    _____

    _____

3. Darren says, "I feel so much better now." What would be your response to him?

    _____

    _____

    _____

4. Andrew says, "The cognitive role play helped me see both the soft side and hard side of me." What might you say to him about what he wants to do with this insight?

    _____

    _____

    _____

5. In the groups you expect to lead, what are some ways you can best help members to consolidate their learnings?

_____

_____

_____

6. What might you say to a member in your group who said he was extremely disappointed in himself for doing so little in the group and remaining safe most of the time?

_____

_____

_____

7. What might you say to a member in your group who said she doubts that people in her life will be as accepting and supportive as the people in the group?

_____

_____

_____

28
Ending Stage

Dealing With Unexpected Conflict

Although conflict most often manifests itself during the transition stage, conflict can occur at any time in the life of a group. Dealing with conflict is not something that is settled once and for all. At the final session, James alludes to a conflict that occurred out of group prior to this meeting, and wonders how people are reacting to him. He quickly wants to sidestep any discussion of the conflict, indicating that maybe later we could talk.

Sensing that there is something in the group that is not being said, Marianne says to James, "Later may be now." She realizes that if the conflict is not addressed, the other pressing business during the ending phase is not likely to be dealt with effectively. The conflict between James and several other members, which occurred outside of the group the night before, was talked about and resolved in this last group session. Misunderstandings were cleared up through dialogue. It didn't take long to address this unfinished business, but it was critical that it was not bypassed.

1. What do you think would occur within the group if the leader decided to ignore an underlying conflict because he or she did not want to stir up things during one of the final sessions?

_____

_____

_____

2. If you sensed some tension between members during a final session, what would be your inclination to say or do?

_____

_____

_____

3. What might you do if members did not seem to be able to resolve a conflicting situation during the final session of a group?

_____

_____

_____

29 Ending Stage

Keeping Members Focused

Marianne announces that we have a different agenda today, meaning that we will be focusing on helping members consolidate their learnings. Marianne says, "We would like for each of you to identify one specific thing that you might carry out of this group into your lives." It is the task of the co-leaders at this time to keep members focused and give all the members a chance to zero in on specific lessons they've acquired. Although only a few sample member comments are shown in the video, typically we structure an ending session in such a manner that everyone has roughly equal time and that nobody gets left out. During both the initial and final sessions, we want to hear all the members' voices.

Another focusing question that we typically raise toward the end of a group is, "Do any of you have any different perceptions now than you did when you first joined this group?" Some of the members' responses are:

Jyl: "I put myself out there and took risks."
Darren: "I see the humanness as I look around this group."
Andrew: "I don't see the masks on people now."
Jackie: "I feel seen and still loved."
Casey: "I'm not rehearsing, and my head doesn't hurt. I'm remembering how afraid I was and how I feel differently now."
Jacqueline: "I'm feeling approved of. Mother is not here in the form of any of you."

1. Assume you were leading this group and one of the members said, "I don't want this group to end. We have become very cohesive and it is a shame to go separate ways. I'd like to see us continue meeting as a group." Would you consider keeping the group together, even if it was announced as a time-limited group?

_____

2. Assume that Jyl was to have said, "I put myself out there and I took risks. Now I am sorry that I did because I feel more vulnerable and won't have any place to go for support." What might you say or do?

_____

_____

_____

3. What would you say to the members of your group about dealing with setbacks once they leave the group?

_____

_____

_____

Noticing Changes and Taking Credit for Them

We encourage members to reflect on what they did in group and how that contributed to what they learned. Once members specify ways they behave differently, they are then in a position to implement this learning in future situations. We also ask members to reflect on how their life might be different if they were to operate on their full power. As one of the members initiates the holding of hands as a closure experience, Marianne asks everyone to look around the room and notice any differences from when the group first convened. Generally, there is a greater sense of cohesion in the group and members feel more connected to others because of the nature of the risks that were taken. There is more identification with one another because of the willingness of members to reveal deeply personal aspects of themselves. The room does indeed feel different. Marianne says, "I hope you remember, not only that you are feeling good and close to one another, but that you remember how you made this happen."

1. If you had been a member of this group, what do you imagine it would have been like for you to terminate this group?

_____

_____

_____

2. Who might you want to stay in contact with, and why?

_____

_____

_____

3. Would you have any concerns about any particular member? Explain.

_____

_____

4. What kind of referrals would you make to the participants?

_____

_____

COREYS' COMMENTARY: THE ENDING STAGE

Much of the focus of this session is on bringing closure to what members did during the weekend. Our central focus is now on assisting members in consolidating their learnings. What you see on the video regarding termination issues is a very small part of that which actually occurred in the group. As a group evolves toward termination, there are a number of tasks that we explore, a few of which include dealing with feelings of separation, dealing with unfinished business, reviewing the group experience, practicing for behavioral change, giving and receiving feedback, talking about ways to carry learnings into life, making contracts of what to do after a group ends, and talking about a follow-up meeting. We remind members again about the importance of maintaining confidentiality. We also ask members to talk about what they might do to discount what they actually did during the group, how they might recover from setbacks, and how to create support systems.

Having completed this self-study program, we want to say that we sincerely hope that it has been a useful and enjoyable process. We hope that you will find ways to continue learning about groups and practicing leadership skills. We want to emphasize that what we consider the single most important element in effective group leadership is your way of being in a group. In the video you saw us utilize a variety of techniques in dealing with the themes that members introduced. Let us stress that we use techniques as means to further the agenda presented to us, not as ends. Techniques are no better than the person using them and are not useful if they are not sensitively adapted to the particular client and context. The outcome of a technique is affected by the climate of the group and by the relationship between the co-leaders and the members. Techniques are merely tools to amplify emerging material that is present and encourage exploration of issues that have personal relevance to the members.

More important than the techniques we use are the attitudes we have toward members, which are manifested by who we are and what we do in the group. When we are fully present and ourselves, we can be a catalyst for members to engage in introspection, relevant self-disclosure, and risk taking. We believe that our primary function as co-leaders is to support members in their journey of making decisions regarding how they want to live. We work with people who are often struggling, who may be lost, or who are experiencing psychological pain. The group experience affords members avenues for finding themselves and enables them to live more peacefully with themselves and others. Sometimes group participants show us their worst. We can be part of the journey as they discover their best.

SUMMARY OF THE ENDING STAGE

Basic Characteristics of the Ending Stage. During the final phase of a group the following characteristics are typically evident:

- Members may pull back and participate in less intense ways, in anticipation of the ending of the group.
- There may be some feelings over the ending of a group as well as fears about being able to implement what they learned in the group.

- Members are encouraged to evaluate the group experience.
- There may be discussion about follow-up meetings or some plan for accountability so that members will be encouraged to carry out their plans for change.

Member Functions. The major task facing members during the final stage of a group is consolidating their learning and transferring what they have learned to their outside environment. Of course, they have been doing this to some extent between sessions if the group has been meeting on a weekly basis. This is the time for them to review the process and outcomes of the entire group and put into some cognitive framework the meaning of the group experience. Some tasks for members at this time are to:

- deal with their feelings about separation and termination
- prepare for generalizing their learning to everyday situations
- give others a better picture of how they are perceived
- complete any unfinished business concerning either issues they have brought into the group or issues that pertain to people in the group
- evaluate the impact of the group
- make decisions and plans concerning what changes they want to make and how they will go about making them

Leader Functions. The group leader's central tasks in the consolidation phase are to provide a structure that allows participants to clarify the meaning of their experiences in the group and to assist members in generalizing their learning from the group to everyday situations. Tasks at this period include:

- assisting members in dealing with any feelings they may have about termination
- giving members an opportunity to express and deal with any unfinished business within the group
- reinforcing changes that members have made and ensuring that members have information about resources to enable them to make further changes
- assisting members in determining how they will apply specific skills in a variety of situations in daily life
- working with members to develop specific contracts and homework assignments as practical ways of making changes
- assisting participants to develop a conceptual framework that will help them understand, integrate, consolidate, and remember what they have learned in the group
- providing opportunities for members to give one another constructive feedback
- reemphasizing the importance of maintaining confidentiality after the group is over

REFERENCES

For a discussion of issues pertaining to the termination of a group experience, characteristics of the ending stage, member and leader functions, and follow-up approaches, see *Groups: Process and Practice* (Chapter 8). For a discussion of techniques for terminating a group, see *Group Techniques* (Chapter 7). For a summary of issues pertaining to the later stages of a group's development, see *Theory and Practice of Group Counseling* (Chapter 5, text and student manual). For a discussion of applying different theoretical perspectives in working with themes emerging from the video group, see *Theory and Practice of Group Counseling* (Chapter 17, text and student manual).

QUESTIONS ON APPLYING THE SUMMARY LIST

Now that you have watched this segment of the group during its ending stage, apply the above summary list to the following questions concerning the video group.

1. What are the *main characteristics* of this group at the ending stage?

_____

_____

_____

2. What *member functions* do you see being illustrated? As you observe the members, what stands out most for you at this phase of the group?

_____

_____

_____

3. Which member (or members) stands out most for you in this segment, and why?

_____

_____

_____

4. What *leader functions* do you see being illustrated? What specific skills and interventions are the co-leaders using at this phase of the group?

_____

_____

_____

5. What are you learning about co-leading a group by observing Marianne and Jerry co-lead this group?

_____

_____

_____

6. What are you learning about how groups either function or malfunction at this point?

_____

_____

_____

Take time to think about a particular kind of group, composed of a specific client population, that you are interested in designing and leading. Answer the following questions from that vantage point.

1. What *specific characteristics* might you expect at the ending stage of the group's development?

    _____

    _____

    _____

2. What *member functions* do you see as being most important at the ending stage?

    _____

    _____

    _____

3. What *leader functions* would you identify as being most crucial at this ending stage?

    _____

    _____

    _____

4. During the ending phase in your group, what are three group leadership skills you see as being especially important? Which of these skills are strong areas for you? Which skills need improvement?

    _____

    _____

    _____

5. What are the *main challenges* you expect to face as your group moves toward termination?

    _____

    _____

    _____

6. If you were co-leading, what would you most want to talk with your co-leader about at the end of your group?

    _____

    _____

    _____

ETHICAL ISSUES IN THE PRACTICE OF GROUP COUNSELING

A mark of professional group leadership is establishing a set of guiding principles. In this section we present some ethical guidelines that are relevant to what you observed on the video and in the workbook discussion of procedures used to facilitate this group. What follows is not a rigid set of policies but, rather, guidelines that can help you clarify your thinking about ways to ensure ethical practice. The purpose in presenting these guidelines is to highlight the ethical dimension that served as a foundation for this group and to stimulate you to think about a framework that will guide you in making sound decisions in the groups you will lead.

1. Think about your needs and behavior styles and about the impact of these factors on group participants. It is essential for you to have a clear idea of what your roles and functions are in the group, so you can communicate them to the members.

2. Have a clear idea of the type of group you are designing. Be able to express the purpose of the group and the characteristics of the clients who will be admitted.

3. Develop a means of screening that will allow you to differentiate between suitable and unsuitable applicants.

4. Consider the advantages of having some kind of pre-group meeting as a way to orient members to a group. The pre-group session is an ideal place to deal with issues pertaining to informed consent.

5. Tell prospective group members what is expected of them. If members know what they are signing up for, the chances are they will be cooperative and become involved group participants. Encourage them to develop a contract that will provide them with the impetus to obtain their personal goals. Inform members that they will be expected to make appropriate self-disclosures, experiment with new behaviors in the group, examine the impact of their interpersonal style on others, express their feelings and thoughts, actively listen to others and attempt to see the world through their eyes, show respect for others, offer genuine support, and try new behaviors outside of the group. It is important that members learn the group norms so they can make maximum use of the group process.

6. Make prospective participants aware of the techniques that will be employed and of the exercises that they may be asked to participate in. Give them the ground rules that will govern group activities.

7. Avoid undertaking a project that is beyond the scope of your training and experience. Make a written statement of your qualifications to conduct a particular group available to the participant.

8. Make clear at the outset of a group what the focus will be. For example, some groups have an educational focus, and so a didactic approach is used. Other groups have a therapeutic focus, and these use an emotive/experiential approach. It is essential that you are clear in your own mind about the purposes of your group and the outcomes members can expect.

9. Protect the members' right to decide what to share with the group and what activities to participate in. Be sensitive to any form of group pressure that violates the self-determination of the participants. Remember that members are more likely to challenge themselves if they are given respect. Invite members to reflect on ways they want to be different and invite them to decide what risks they are willing to take in the group situation.

10. Develop a rationale for using group interventions, and be able to verbalize it. Use only those interventions and techniques that you are competent to employ. It is best if you have experienced as a member the techniques you use.

11. Relate practice to theory, and remain open to integrating multiple approaches into your practice. Be thoroughly grounded in a number of diverse theoretical orientations as a basis for creating your own personalized style of leading groups.

12. Be aware of the cultural context as you work with members. Be willing to adapt your techniques based on the members' cultural values and cultural background.

13. Be willing to discuss with members the psychological risks involved in group participation both before they enter and also when it is appropriate throughout the life of the group. Members may need to explore the risks involved in translating what they are learning in group to everyday life.

14. Emphasize the importance of confidentiality to members before they enter a group, during the group sessions when relevant, and before the group terminates. Realize that confidentiality is essential for trust to develop.

15. When it is appropriate, be open with the group about your values, but avoid imposing them on clients. Recognize the role that the members' culture and socialization play in the formulation of their values. Respect your clients' capacity to think for themselves, and be sure that members give one another the same respect.

16. Make referral resources available to people who need or desire further psychological assistance. Help members to formulate plans for continuing their self-understanding once the group is over.

17. Encourage participants to discuss their experience in the group and help them evaluate the degree to which they are meeting their personal goals.

18. Do not expect the transfer of learning from the group to daily life to occur automatically. Assist members in applying what they have learned in the group situation to life outside of group. Prepare them for possible setbacks.

19. Schedule a follow-up session so members are able to see how others in their group have done and so you have a basis for evaluating the impact on the group experience.

20. Develop some method of evaluation to determine the effectiveness of your interventions in the group.

At this point, you have most likely watched the video a number of times and you have involved yourself in the discussions and exercises in this workbook. You might want to watch the video one more time, paying special attention to any possible ethical issues involved with this group. Take the time to react to the questions below, especially from the vantage point of applying ethical guidelines to a group you may want to design and lead.

1. What are some of the most important lessons you have learned from watching this video and studying this workbook pertaining to what it means to become an ethical group practitioner?

_____

_____

_____

2. What ethical issues do you think are involved in co-leading a group?

_____

_____

_____

3. What do you think it will take for you to become a competent group practitioner?

_____

_____

_____

4. From an ethical perspective, what is your role in understanding how diversity can operate in a group? What have you learned about working with diversity from an ethical vantage point?

_____

_____

_____

5. What ethical issues would you consider in getting members for one of your groups?

_____

_____

_____

6. How would you go about making sure that members would be able to give their informed consent in a group you were leading?

_____

_____

_____

7. What would you most want to tell members about confidentiality?

_____

_____

_____

8. What ethical considerations do you think are involved in challenging members to talk about their resistances and ways they may hold back in a group?

_____

_____

_____

9. How ready are you to assist members in exploring the kinds of personal issues that you observed in the video? To what degree have you been willing to explore your personal concerns?

_____

_____

_____

10. What is one step you can take to increase the likelihood of becoming an effective and ethical group practitioner?

_____

_____

_____

FOLLOW-UP SELF-INVENTORY

Now that you have worked through all the stages in the evolution of this group in conjunction with the workbook, we suggest that you take this inventory to determine how any of your perspectives on group process may have changed. Use the following code:

5 = I *strongly agree* with this statement.
4 = I *agree*, in most respects, with this statement.
3 = I am *undecided* in my opinion about this statement.
2 = I *disagree*, in most respects, with this statement.
1 = I *strongly disagree* with this statement.

_____ 1. To create a sense of trust among the members, I would be inclined to ask members to talk about any reservations they have pertaining to the safety of the room.

_____ 2. Confidentiality needs to be taught to group members and monitored during the life of a group.

_____ 3. Early in the course of a group, one of my main tasks is to assist members in formulating specific personal goals.

_____ 4. If I become emotionally involved in a group as the leader, then I certainly lose my objectivity, which restricts my effectiveness.

_____ 5. I see it as essential that I am willing to engage in appropriate self-disclosure, even though I am facilitating the group.

_____ 6. I prefer co-leading a group to leading alone.

_____ 7. Resistance in a member or in the group as a whole is generally due to inept group leadership.

_____ 8. Conflict among or between members and leaders is usually a destructive element indicating that cohesion is absent within the group.

_____ 9. If members express fears related to participating in the group, it is generally a good idea for others to quickly provide a great deal of reassurance.

_____ 10. Once trust is established in a group it is rarely necessary to reestablish trust at a later time.

_____ 11. There are clear demarcations between each of the stages of a group.

_____ 12. Leader confrontation of members should be avoided at all costs until the group has reached a working stage.

_____ 13. A sign of a working stage is a willingness on the part of members to spontaneously involve themselves in interactions within the group.

_____ 14. If my group does not reach a working stage, this is a sign that very little learning has taken place.

_____ 15. Unless most of the members of a group have expressed intense emotions, it can hardly be said that this group has achieved a working stage.

_____ 16. There is a fine line between the transition and the working stage.

_____ 17. Linking one member to another member and asking each of them to talk directly to each other typically is very unproductive.

_____ 18. Role-playing in group is generally fairly artificial and usually creates a good deal of resistance in members.

_____ 19. Facilitating members to focus on their awareness of here-and-now reactions is a useful way to create a trusting climate.

_____ 20. Once the group reaches a working stage, group leaders are really not necessary.

_____ 21. Therapeutic work with a member that is characterized by a good deal of emotional release typically leads to insight without expecting members to do any cognitive processing.

_____ 22. Members can frequently create an agenda for their personal work in a group by paying attention to how others affect them and sharing their reactions with others.

_____ 23. The use of contracts is an effective way of helping members put an action plan into operation outside of the group.

_____ 24. It is important to give members an opportunity to deal with unfinished business within the group toward the ending phase.

_____ 25. I would structure some final sessions so that each member both gives and receives feedback.

_____ 26. Members will learn more from a group experience if I help them practice interpersonal skills toward the ending phase of group.

_____ 27. In designing techniques for group facilitation, it is essential to consider the client's cultural background.

_____ 28. Any leader countertransference is a clear indication that he or she is unable to effectively lead a group.

_____ 29. The most important aspect of being a competent group leader is the ability to apply leadership skills.

_____ 30. The group leader's willingness to use him/herself as a therapeutic instrument is of the utmost importance.

Go over this inventory and circle the numbers of items where you think the greatest degree of learning has occurred. What specific modifications have you seen in your views on groups? Write down a few lessons that stand out for you.

_____

_____

_____

_____

_____

_____

Having completed the above follow-up inventory, go back to the **Pretest** and **Posttest** that you took at the beginning of this self-study program. We recommend that you take the time to re-take this inventory, comparing your responses now to the first time you took the inventory. This posttest will be a helpful way to review key points in the program and it will assist you in identifying ways that you may have increased your awareness of group process and group facilitation. From viewing the video, reading the textbook, participating in discussions in your class or group, and involving yourself in the self-study material in this workbook, what are the major shifts that have occurred in your thinking about group counseling and group leadership?

_____

_____

_____

_____

_____

_____

_____

_____

_____

_____

_____

_____

SOME FINAL THOUGHTS

As you participated in this self-study on group process, we hope that you were able to appreciate that group facilitation involves far more than applying techniques or solving problems. As you have seen, being in a group is a deeply personal experience for both the members and the co-leaders.

The video that you watched and studied is a unique educational endeavor, since the group members are being themselves, rather than enacting a predetermined script. As we mentioned at the beginning of this workbook, it is difficult to watch this video in a purely objective and detached fashion. The chances are that as you watched sections of this video you became emotionally involved because the participants were exploring universal themes that connect us in the human condition. If you were affected personally as you reviewed the tape, we think that this is an opportunity to seek some therapeutic paths to explore your own feelings and thoughts. When you work with clients you will most likely be affected by certain problems they bring up or with emotions they express.

Before we left the group room, we invited the "crew" (camera operators, production assistant, light and sound technicians, director, and producer) to express what it was like for them to be on the outside as the group was working for three days. The crew members reported that they typically are not affected by the content of the videotaping because they are fully occupied attending to the technical work they are doing. In this situation, all reported being affected and several reported becoming tearful at times as a result of the group discussion. Other crew members reported that they found themselves drawn into the issues being discussed which forced them to think about their own history, families, and experiences and reexamine their values regarding these issues.

WHERE ARE YOU NOW AND
WHERE WILL YOU GO FROM HERE?

As a final exercise, we ask you to reflect on what have been the significant learnings for you from viewing the video and completing the workbook and to clarify where you want to go from here.

1. How has your view of group counseling changed after viewing the video and completing the activities in this workbook?

_____

_____

_____

_____

_____

_____
_____
_____
_____
_____
_____

2. What are some of your major learnings regarding how to become an effective group member?

_____
_____
_____
_____
_____
_____
_____
_____
_____
_____

3. What are some major things you learned about yourself as a person, and how this is likely to influence your work as a group counselor?

_____
_____
_____
_____
_____
_____
_____
_____
_____

4. What are the key lessons you have learned about leading a group?

_____
_____

_____

_____

_____

_____

_____

_____

_____

_____

_____

5. Think about what you have seen on the video and summarize the ethical issues. What ethical considerations can you think of that pertain to the evolution of a group? What are some ethical considerations you would want to reflect upon as you design and lead a group?

_____

_____

_____

_____

_____

_____

_____

_____

_____

_____

6. What are some questions that viewing the video and completing the workbook have raised for you?

_____

_____

_____

_____

_____

_____

_____

_____

_____

_____

7. Where will you go from here as you work toward your development as an effective group counselor?

_____

_____

_____

_____

_____

_____

_____

_____

_____

_____

_____

ANNOTATED TEXTS AS COMPANIONS WITH THIS VIDEO

All of the following group books can be used in conjunction with the *Evolution of a Group* video and workbook, and all these books can be useful in furthering your understanding of group process.

Corey, G. (2000). *Theory and Practice of Group Counseling* (5th ed.). Belmont, CA: Brooks/Cole • Wadsworth. [and Student Manual].

This text covers ten major theoretical approaches to group work. The book and manual also deal with topics such as: ethics in group, group leadership, stages of group, and developing an integrative perspective. Chapter 17 consists of a case illustration based on the video, *Evolution of a Group.*

Corey, G., Corey, M. S., Callanan, P., & Russell, J. M. (1992). *Group Techniques* (2nd ed.). Pacific Grove, CA: Brooks/Cole.

Describes ideas for creating and implementing techniques for use in groups. Gives a rationale for the use of techniques in all the stages in a group's development. This book also fits well with the video, *Evolution of a Group,* since the book describes designing techniques at each of the various stages of group.

Corey, M. S., & Corey, G. (1997). *Groups: Process and Practice* (5th ed.). Pacific Grove, CA: Brooks/Cole.

Outlines the basic issues and concepts of group process throughout the life history of a group. Applies these basic concepts to groups for children, adolescents, adults, and the elderly. Chapters 1 through 8 are especially relevant for the group video, since these chapters deal with all of the stages of group.

Donigian, J., & Hulse-Killacky, D. (1999). *Critical Incidents in Group Therapy* (2nd ed.). Pacific Grove, CA: Brooks/Cole.

> In this excellent book the group therapists, each a proponent of a different theoretical orientation, respond to six critical incidents in group therapy. They explain the thinking they went through to determine their particular responses to the incident. The book covers 12 theories.

Donigian, J., & Malnati, R. (1997). *Systemic Group Therapy: A Triadic Model.* Pacific Grove, CA: Brooks/Cole.

> Part III of this group deals with these stages of group: orientation, conflict and confrontation, cohesiveness, work, and termination. This book also deals with interventions leaders can use, which makes it useful to use in conjunction with the video.

Jacobs, E. E., Masson, R. L., & Harvill, R. L. (1998). *Group Counseling: Strategies and Skills* (3rd. ed.). Pacific Grove, CA: Brooks/Cole.

> This group text covers a number of topical areas generally covered in most group courses such as stages of groups, planning, getting started, skills and exercises, leading during the middle stages of a group, closing a session, and dealing with problem situations.

Kottler, J. A. (1994). *Advanced Group Leadership.* Pacific Grove, CA: Brooks/Cole.

> Kottler addresses a number of topics in his text that would be useful reading as a supplement to the group video. Some of these topics are working with difficult group members, productive risk taking, use of humor in groups, the power of language in groups, and compatible co-leader functioning.

Shapiro, J. L., Peltz, L. S., & Bernadett-Shapiro, S. (1998). *Brief Group Treatment: Practical Training for Therapists and Counselors.* Pacific Grove, CA: Brooks/Cole.

> Much of this book is geared to stages of groups. Separate chapters are devoted to these phases: preparation, transition, treatment, and termination.

Yalom, I. D. (1995). *The Theory and Practice of Group Psychotherapy.* NY: Basic Books.

> Yalom has a comprehensive discussion of the advantages of working in the here-and-now and covers a range of clinical issues in working with problem group members and specialized group formats. There is much in this book that would work well with the group video.

OTHER BOOKS BY THE COREYS

The following are other books that the Coreys have authored or co-authored that might be of interest to you. All of these except *Living and Learning* are published by the Brooks/Cole Publishing Company, Pacific Grove, California 93950.

Corey, M. S., & Corey, G. (1998). *Becoming a Helper* (3rd ed.).

> This book deals with topics of concern to students who are studying in one of the helping professions. Some of the issues explored are examining your motivations and needs, becoming aware of the impact of your values on the counseling process, learning to cope with stress, dealing with burnout, exploring developmental turning points in one's life, and ethical issues.

Corey, G., Corey, M. S., & Callanan, P. (1998). *Issues and Ethics in the Helping Professions* (5th ed.).

A combination textbook and student manual that contains self-inventories, open-ended cases and problem situations, exercises, suggested activities, and a variety of ethical, professional, and legal issues facing practitioners.

Corey, G., & Corey, M. S. (1997). *I Never Knew I Had a Choice* (6th ed.).

A self-help book for personal growth that deals with topics such as the struggle to achieve autonomy; the roles that work, sex roles, sexuality, love, intimacy, and solitude play in our lives; the meaning of loneliness, death, and loss; and the ways in which we choose values and find meaning in life.

Corey, G., Corey, C., & Corey, H. (1997). *Living and Learning*. Belmont, CA: Wadsworth.

Presents learning as a lifelong journey. By encouraging readers to use the world as their classroom and to "learn from living," this book helps readers to get more out of their college experience and the rest of their lives.

Corey, G. (1996). *Theory and Practice of Counseling and Psychotherapy* (5th ed.).

Presents an overview of nine contemporary theories of counseling, with an emphasis on the practical applications and the therapeutic process associated with each orientation. And *Student Manual for Theory and Practice of Counseling and Psychotherapy* (5th ed.).

Corey, G. (1996). *Case Approach to Counseling and Psychotherapy* (4th ed.)

Designed to demonstrate how theory can be applied to specific cases. Readers are challenged to apply their knowledge of theories to a variety of cases. Dr. Corey demonstrates his way of working with these cases from each of nine theoretical perspectives and also in an eclectic, integrated fashion.

EVALUATION FORM

To the owner of this video and workbook:

We hope that, as you viewed *Evolution of a Group* and used this Student Workbook that accompanied the video, you found that your readings of group process have come more to life. Only through your comments can we assess how this learning package was used and the meaning it had for you.

School and address _____

_____

Instructor's name _____

1. In what class did you use this video and workbook?

_____

2. If applicable, check which book you used for the course:

    _____ *Theory and Practice of Group Counseling* (Gerald Corey)
    _____ *Groups: Process and Practice* (Marianne Schneider Corey and Gerald Corey)
    _____ *Group Techniques* (Gerald Corey, Marianne Schneider Corey, Patrick Callanan, and J. Michael Russell).

    Other (please specify title and author) _____

_____

3. How did you use the combination of this video and Student Workbook?

_____

_____

4. What did you like *most* about this video and the workbook?

_____

_____

_____

5. What did you like *least* about this video and the workbook?

_____

_____

_____

6. How useful were the group sessions in helping you learn how to facilitate a group?

_____

_____

_____

_____

_____

7. In the space below, please write any other comments about the video and workbook that you would like to make. We welcome and appreciate your suggestions! Please mail comments to:

Brooks/Cole • Wadsworth
511 Forest Lodge Road
Pacific Grove, California 93950-9968